200 Light
weekday meals

200 Light

weekday meals

hamlyn **all color**

An Hachette UK Company
www.hachette.co.uk

First published in Great Britain in 2015 by Hamlyn
a division of Octopus Publishing Group Ltd,
Endeavour House, 189 Shaftesbury Avenue,
London, WC2H 8JY
www.octopusbooks.co.uk

Distributed in the US by Hachette Book Group
1290 Avenue of the Americas, 4th and 5th Floors
New York, NY 10020

Distributed in Canada by Canadian Manda Group
664 Annette St., Toronto, Ontario, Canada M6S 2C8

ISBN: 978-0-600-62971-9
Printed and bound in China

10 9 8 7 6 5 4 3 2 1

Standard level kitchen cup and spoon measurements are
used in all recipes

Ovens should be preheated to the specified temperature;
if using a convection oven, follow the manufacturer's
instructions for adjusting the time and temperature.

Fresh herbs, large eggs, and freshly ground black pepper
should be used unless otherwise stated.

This book includes dishes made with nuts and nut
derivatives. It is advisable for people with known allergic
reactions to nuts and nut derivatives or those who may be
potentially vulnerable to these allergies, such as pregnant
and nursing mothers, people with a weakened immune sys-
tem, the elderly, babies, and children, to avoid dishes made
with these. It is prudent to check the labels of all prepared
ingredients for the possible inclusion of nut derivatives.

contents

Introduction

introduction

this series

The Hamlyn All Color Light Series is a collection of handy-sized books, each packed with over 200 healthy recipes on a variety of topics and cuisines to suit your needs.

The books are designed to help those people who are trying to lose weight by offering a range of delicious recipes that are low in calories but still high in flavor. The recipes shows the calorie count per portion, so you will know exactly what you are eating. These are recipes for real and delicious food, not ultra-slimming meals, so they will help you maintain your new, healthier eating plan for life. They must be used as part of a balanced diet, with the cakes and sweet dishes eaten only as an occasional treat.

how to use this book

All the recipes in this book are clearly marked with the number of calories (kcal) per serving. The chapters cover different calorie bands: under 500 calories, under 400 calories, etc.

There are variations of each recipe at the bottom of the page—note the calorie count as they do vary and can sometimes be more than the original recipe.

The figures assume that you are using low-fat versions of dairy products, so be sure to use skim milk and low-fat yogurt. They have also been calculated using lean meat, so make sure you trim meat of all visible fat and remove the skin from chicken breasts. Use moderate amounts of oil and butter for cooking and low-fat/low-calorie alternatives when you can.

Don't forget to take note of the number of portions each recipe makes and divide up the quantity of food accordingly, so that you know exactly how many calories you are consuming. Be careful about side dishes and accompaniments as they will add to the calorie content.

Above all, enjoy trying out the new flavors and exciting recipes that this book contains. Rather than dwelling on the thought that you are denying yourself your usual unhealthy treats, think of your new regime as a positive step toward a new you. Not only will you lose weight and feel more confident, but your health will benefit, the condition of your hair and nails will improve, and you will take on a healthy glow.

the risks of obesity

Up to half of women and two-thirds of men are overweight or obese in the developed world today. Being overweight not only can make us unhappy with our appearance, but can also lead to serious health problems, including heart disease, high blood pressure, and diabetes.

When someone is obese, it means they are overweight to the point that it could start to seriously threaten their health. In fact, obesity ranks as a close second to smoking as a possible cause of cancer. Obese women are more likely to have complications during and after pregnancy, and people who are overweight or obese are also more likely to suffer from coronary heart disease, gallstones, osteoarthritis, high blood pressure, and type 2 diabetes.

how can I tell if I am overweight?

The best way to tell if you are overweight is to work out your body mass index (BMI). If using metric measurements, divide your weight in kilograms (kg) by your height in meters (m) squared. (For example, if you are 1.7 m tall and weigh 70 kg, the calculation would be $70 \div 2.89 = 24.2$.) If using imperial measurements, divide your weight in pounds (lb) by your height in inches (in) squared and

multiply by 703. Then compare the figure to the list below (these figures apply to healthy adults only).

Less than 20	underweight
20–25	healthy
25–30	overweight
Over 30	obese

As we all know by now, one of the major causes of obesity is eating too many calories.

what is a calorie?

Our bodies need energy to stay alive, grow, keep warm, and be active. We get the energy we need to survive from the food and drinks we consume—more specifically, from the fat, carbohydrate, protein, and alcohol that they contain.

A calorie (cal), as anyone who has ever been on a diet will know, is the unit used to measure how much energy different foods contain. A calorie can be scientifically defined as the energy required to raise the temperature of 1 gram of water from 58.1°F to 59.9°F. A kilocalorie (kcal) is 1,000 calories and it is, in fact, kilocalories that we usually mean when we talk about the calories in different foods.

Different food types contain different numbers of calories. For example, a gram of carbohydrate (starch or sugar) provides 3.75 kcal, protein provides 4 kcal per gram, fat provides 9 kcal per gram, and alcohol provides 7 kcal per gram. So, fat is the most concentrated source of energy—weight for weight, it provides just over twice as many calories as either protein or carbohydrate —with alcohol not far behind. The energy content of a food or drink depends on how many grams of carbohydrate, fat, protein, and alcohol are present.

how many calories do we need?

The number of calories we need to consume varies from person to person, but your body weight is a clear indication of whether you are eating the right amount. Body weight is simply determined by the number of calories you are eating compared to the number of calories your body is using to maintain itself and needed for physical activity. If you regularly consume more calories than you use up, you will start to gain weight as extra energy is stored in the body as fat.

Based on our relatively inactive modern-day lifestyles, most nutritionists recommend that women should aim to consume around 2,000

calories (kcal) per day, and men an amount of around 2,500. Of course, the amount of energy required depends on your level of activity: the more active you are, the more energy you need to maintain a stable weight.

a healthier lifestyle

To maintain a healthy body weight, we need to expend as much energy as we eat; to lose weight, energy expenditure must therefore exceed intake of calories. So, exercise is a vital tool in the fight to lose weight. Physical activity doesn't just help us control body weight; it also helps to reduce our appetite and is known to have beneficial effects on the heart and blood that help prevent against cardiovascular disease.

Many of us claim we don't enjoy exercise and simply don't have the time to fit it into our hectic schedules, so the easiest way to increase physical activity is by incorporating it into our daily routines, perhaps by walking or cycling instead of driving (particularly for short journeys), taking up more active hobbies such as gardening, and taking small and simple steps, such as using the stairs instead of the elevator whenever possible.

As a general guide, adults should aim to undertake at least 30 minutes of moderate-intensity exercise, such as a brisk walk, five times a week. The 30 minutes does not have to be taken all at once: three sessions of 10 minutes are equally beneficial. Children and young people should be encouraged to take

at least 60 minutes of moderate-intensity exercise every day.

Some activities will use up more energy than others. The following list shows some examples of the energy a person weighing 132 lb would expend doing the following activities for 30 minutes:

activity	energy
Ironing	69 kcal
Cleaning	75 kcal
Walking	99 kcal
Golf	129 kcal
Fast walking	150 kcal
Cycling	180 kcal
Aerobics	195 kcal
Swimming	195 kcal
Running	300 kcal
Sprinting	405 kcal

make changes for life

The best way to lose weight is to try to adopt healthier eating habits that you can easily maintain all the time, not just when you are trying to slim down. Aim to lose no more than 2 lb per week to ensure you lose only your fat stores. People who go on crash diets lose lean muscle as well as fat and are much more likely to put the weight back on again soon afterward.

For a woman, the aim is to reduce her daily calorie intake to around 1,500 kcal while she is trying to lose weight, then settle on around 2,000 per day thereafter to maintain her new body weight. Regular exercise will also make a huge difference: the more you can burn, the less you will need to diet.

improve your diet

For most of us, simply adopting a more balanced diet will reduce our calorie intake and lead to weight loss. Follow these simple recommendations:

Eat more starchy foods, such as bread, potatoes, rice, and pasta. Assuming these replace the fattier foods you usually eat, and you don't smother them with oil or butter, this will help reduce the amount of fat and increase the amount of fiber in your diet. As a bonus, try to use wholegrain rice, pasta, and flour, as the energy from these foods is released more slowly in the body, making you feel fuller for longer.

Eat more fruit and vegetables, aiming for at least 9 portions of different fruit and vegetables a day (excluding potatoes). As long as you don't add extra fat to your fruit and vegetables in the form of cream, butter, or oil, these changes will help reduce your fat intake and increase the amount of fiber and vitamins you consume.

Eat fewer sugary foods, such as cookies, cakes, and candy bars. This will also help reduce your fat intake. If you fancy something sweet, aim for fresh or dried fruit instead.

Reduce the amount of fat in your diet, so you consume fewer calories. Choosing low-fat versions of dairy products, such as skim milk and low-fat yogurt, doesn't necessarily mean your food will be tasteless. Low-fat versions are available for most dairy products, including milk, cheese, crème fraîche, yogurt, and even cream and butter.

Choose lean cuts of meat, such as Canadian bacon instead of regular bacon, and chicken breasts instead of thighs. Trim all visible fat off meat before cooking and avoid frying foods—grill or roast instead. Fish is also naturally low in fat and can make a variety of tempting dishes.

simple steps to reduce your intake:

Few of us have an iron will, so when you are trying to cut down make it easier on yourself by following these steps:

- Serve small portions to start with. You may feel satisfied when you have finished, but if you are still hungry you can always go back for more.
- Once you have served up your meal, put away any leftover food before you eat. Don't put full serving dishes on the table as you will undoubtedly pick, even if you feel satisfied with what you have already eaten.
- Eat slowly and savor your food; then you are more likely to feel full when you have finished. If you rush a meal, you may still feel hungry afterward.
- Make an effort with your meals. Just because you are cutting down doesn't mean your meals have to be low on taste as well as calories. You will feel more satisfied with a meal you have really enjoyed and will be less likely to look for comfort in a bag of potato chips or a bar of chocolate.
- Plan your meals in advance to make sure you have all the ingredients you need. Searching the pantry when you are hungry is unlikely to result in a healthy, balanced meal.
- Keep healthy and interesting snacks at hand for those moments when you need something to pep you up. You don't need to succumb to a chocolate bar if there are other tempting treats on offer.

weekday meals

When we stop to think about our modern lives, it's easy to see how meals can get pushed into the background and be made to fit around our other commitments. Time is in such short supply that most of us scarcely have time to eat our meals, let alone plan them, shop for them and cook them. That is why we have included the recipes in this book, which bring together some delicious and nutritious dishes that all the family can enjoy together and that will only take a short time to prepare and cook.

For many, cooking in the week is a bore; it is a "must-do" activity rather than a "like-to." Energy and creativity levels are low, there's very little time and there are other things you need to be getting on with. So we have come

up with this book to put the pleasure back into cooking meals midweek. We believe that no matter how little time you have, cooking should be a creative, therapeutic, enjoyable process with an end result you can be proud of. But we are realistic; we know time is tight; there is paperwork to do after dinner and the house needs cleaning before your guests arrive tomorrow.

take time to plan healthy balanced meals

Some "food in a hurry"-style cook books assume you have an army of helpers in your kitchen and an array of special gadgets and equipment to speed up the prep process. We make no such assumptions. We do however hope that you will take a little time to plan and buy for your dishes because the key to midweek meal success is preparation. Use some of your lunch-hour or some time at the weekend to browse through this book and choose four or five meals that you'd like to serve in the week. Then once you've worked out what ingredients you need, ensure you get everything in stock ready for the beginning of the week. Don't forget internet shopping and home-delivery services—they are designed for busy people and can be arranged for times that suit you and your busy schedule.

mix it up

It may seem obvious, but when you are planning your week's meals, try to get a good balance of different foods on your plate each day and through the week. We have planned the recipes in this book to help give you a broad range of nutrient-dense foods across the week, but the key is to mix up your menus and not always cook the same types of food. We would suggest that you bear the following in mind when you are creating your meal plan:

- Eat fish at least twice a week as it is known to reduce heart disease, is rich in B and D vitamins, and contains high levels of Omega 3 which is great for your heart.

- Chicken can be eaten as often as your budget allows, but try to afford organic where possible.

- If you are a red-meat addict, choose lean cuts where possible and cuts which lend themselves to quick cooking. Limit red meat to twice a week.

- Offal is an excellent source of vitamins, copper, iron, and zinc, however, as the liver tends to accumulate chemical residues from the animal, limit your intake to once a week.

- Nuts and seeds are nutritional gems. They are low in saturated fats, high in protein and fiber, and are brimming with B vitamins and many useful minerals.

- Eggs are a quick and healthy protein source and low in saturated fat—current thinking is that up to 6 eggs per week is a perfectly healthy addition to your diet.

- Mix up your vegetables as much as your budget allows. Include root and leafy veg

and as many different colors as you can. All vegetables contain high levels of vitamin C, many contain important B vitamins, and all are abundant in fiber. What's more, when they are cooked lightly and quickly as many are in this book, their goodness is retained and their benefits are felt all the more.

- Always choose wholegrains as these are good for your heart and keep you fuller for longer.

a well-stocked kitchen

It helps if you keep your kitchen well stocked at all times so you only have to buy the fresh and one-off ingredients each week. For those who keep their pantries quite lean, this can be a rather time-consuming and possibly expensive exercise initially, but it is worth it to keep costs down thereafter and to reduce time spent shopping each week.

Don't be afraid to buy some "cheat" ingredients for those super-quick meals you're going to prepare; pesto sauces, ready-made pizza bases and Thai curry paste are must-haves for busy days, plus remember you can buy garlic, ginger, and lemon grass in paste-form that can be quickly and easily squeezed into the pan when cooking.

Jars of preserved vegetables are a tasty, easy addition to many pastas, salads, and rice dishes and can be stored for months, if not years, very successfully as long as they are kept cool. Therefore it would not go amiss to treat yourself to some jars of artichokes, olives, and roasted red peppers, and to add the occasional kick to your cooking, keep some capers and anchovies in stock too; you'd surprised how much these tiny additions add to a meal.

You may not think of yourself as a gardener, but learning to keep a few potted herbs on the windowsill will benefit you no end when it comes to adding quick and easy flavor to a midweek meal. Easy-to-keep herbs include basil, cilantro, chives, and rosemary. Oregano and thyme can be a little trickier to keep, however these can be bought fresh in bunches and frozen for when you need them. Don't be concerned if the leaves go very dark or black—they will retain their flavor.

the fridge and freezer

Make space in your fridge for some key ingredients that form the basis for many meals: onions, garlic, hard cheese, a good

To whiz up a magical meal in minutes, you are going to need some basics in your kitchen. All-purpose flour and cornstarch and a bottle of UHT milk for making emergency sauces, cans of diced tomatoes, chickpeas and beans, tomato sauce, tomato paste, strong English mustard, a good selection of oils including a basic vegetable oil such as sunflower oil, a good quality olive oil, and some more alternative flavors such as groundnut, sesame, and walnut. Always have a good quality balsamic vinegar in the pantry, and for those dishes with an oriental twist, stock up on coconut milk, soy sauce, fish sauce, sweet chili dipping sauce, hoi sin, plus a selection of your preferred noodles and rice.

strong Parmesan, and some plain yogurt. Keep quartered lemons and limes, ginger, and chilies in the freezer, plus nutrient-rich veggies that freeze well such as spinach, peas, or corn. Bacon, chicken and fish fillets, and sausages can be separated and frozen in small servings ready for easy defrosting, or buy bags of frozen shrimp, mussels, or mixed seafood for an easy addition to soups, stews, and stir-fries.

When a loaf of bread is no longer fresh enough to eat in slices, whiz up the loaf in a food processor and freeze the bread crumbs in small food bags ready for coating your chicken or fish fillets. Remember, too, that bread freezes well and bags of muffins and burger buns kept in the freezer are sure to get good use.

short cuts

If you do not have a microwave and have forgotten to take meat, poultry or fish out of the freezer, you can speed up the process of defrosting by immersing the wrapped frozen food in a sink of cold water and leaving it for a couple of hours.

Instead of crushing garlic, chop the end off a clove and grate it instead. It saves time washing up the garlic crusher and wastes less of the clove. If the recipe requires a large number of garlic cloves, you can save time by adding garlic paste straight from the tube. The flavor is intense, so take care: you need only a small amount to replace a clove of garlic.

Fresh cilantro is a wonderful herb, which adds huge amounts of flavor to all sorts of dishes. Make sure you always have the flavor of "fresh cilantro" by keeping a store of pots or tubes of cilantro paste, which preserves the cilantro leaves in a mixture of oil and vinegar. Alternatively, freeze a bunch of fresh cilantro in a freezer bag ready to crumble into your cooking. Freezing will blacken the leaves and only marginally reduce the fresh cilantro taste.

fast food that's good for you

Whether you are young or old, a vegetarian or an omnivore, we all need much the same nutrients from the food we eat. Our energy comes from food and fluids, and if we are to get the full and complete range of nutrients that our bodies need we should be consuming carbohydrates, protein, fats, fiber, and water as well as a variety of vitamins and minerals. These nutrients not only fuel our bodies, but many of them also actually improve our health and help protect us against diseases. If we eat well, we feel well, our mood is improved, and we can cope better with stress—which can only be a good thing if we're running a busy household.

When you have tried some of the recipes in this book, we sincerely hope you rediscover the joys of midweek cooking. Yes, life is busy, there is always a mountain of jobs that need to be done, but cooking your midweek meal is one job that can be enjoyable, creative, and rewarding. So pick a recipe and get cooking! You could find yourself calmer, happier, and satisfied in more ways than one!

recipes
under 200
calories

black sesame seeds with shrimp

Calories per serving **132**

Serves **4 (with 2 other main dishes)**

Preparation time **10 minutes**

Cooking time **about 10 minutes**

½ tablespoon **black sesame seeds**

1½ tablespoons **sunflower oil**

2–3 **garlic cloves**, finely chopped

8 oz **raw shrimp**, peeled and deveined

1 cup **water chestnuts**, drained and thinly sliced

1½ cups **snow peas**, trimmed

2 tablespoons **vegetable stock**, **seafood stock**, or **water**

1 tablespoon **light soy sauce**

1 tablespoon **oyster sauce**

Dry-fry the black sesame seeds in a small pan for 1–2 minutes or until they are fragrant, then set them aside.

Heat the oil in a wok or large skillet and stir-fry the garlic over medium heat until it is lightly browned.

Add the shrimp, water chestnuts, and snow peas and stir-fry over high heat for 1–2 minutes. Add the stock, soy sauce, and oyster sauce and stir-fry for another 2–3 minutes or until the shrimp open and turn pink. Stir in the fried sesame seeds and serve immediately.

For homemade seafood stock, put 7 cups cold water, 1 onion (outer skins removed, root cut off, quartered), 1 carrot (coarsely chopped), 3 garlic cloves (unpeeled, lightly bruised), 8 inches lemon grass stalks (bruised, coarsely sliced), 1 inch piece of fresh ginger root (peeled, finely sliced), 3 whole cilantro plants (cleaned, the roots lightly bruised), 30 sundried goji berries (optional), and 5 black peppercorns in a large pot. Heat over medium heat to boiling point. Reduce to low heat and simmer for 10 minutes. During simmering, skim from time to time. Add 8 oz fish heads, tails, and bones (cleaned) or mixed fish bones and shrimp shells, simmering for another 10–15 minutes. Strain the stock into a clean bowl. **Calories per serving 132**

20

peppered beef with salad greens

Calories per serving **148**
Serves **6**
Preparation time **20 minutes**
Cooking time **4–7 minutes**

2 **thick-cut sirloin steaks**,
about 1 lb in total
3 teaspoons **colored**
peppercorns, coarsely
crushed
coarse salt flakes
¾ cup **plain yogurt**
1–1½ teaspoons **horseradish**
sauce (to taste)
1 **garlic clove**, crushed
4 cups **mixed salad greens**
1½ cups sliced **button**
mushrooms
1 **red onion**, thinly sliced
1 tablespoon **olive oil**
salt and **pepper**

Trim the fat from the steaks and rub the meat with the crushed peppercorns and salt flakes.

Mix together the yogurt, horseradish sauce, and garlic and season to taste with salt and pepper. Add the salad greens, mushrooms, and most of the red onion and toss together gently.

Heat the oil in a skillet, add the steaks and cook over high heat for 2 minutes, until browned. Turn over and cook for 2 minutes for medium rare, 3–4 minutes for medium, or 5 minutes for well done.

Spoon the salad greens into the center of six serving plates. Thinly slice the steaks and arrange the pieces on top, then garnish with the remaining red onion.

For lemon beef with mustard dressing, trim the steaks and season with salt and a light grinding of black pepper. Make the salad as above, replacing the yogurt with ¾ cup half-fat crème fraîche or sour cream and using 2 tablespoons whole-grain mustard instead of the horseradish. Cook the steaks as above, adding the juice of ½ lemon to the skillet after removing the steaks from the heat. Turn the steaks in the lemon a couple of times, then serve as above. **Calories per serving 219**

mussels in black bean sauce

Calories per serving **129**
Serves **4 as an appetizer**
Preparation time **15 minutes**
Cooking time **7 minutes**

2 lb **live mussels**
1 tablespoon **peanut oil**
2 **garlic cloves**, finely sliced
2 tablespoons **black bean
  sauce**
1 tablespoon **chopped fresh
  ginger root**
2 tablespoons **Chinese rice
  wine** or **dry sherry**
1 tablespoon **light soy sauce**
4 tablespoons **water**
handful of **cilantro leaves**,
  coarsely chopped

Scrub the mussels thoroughly under cold running water. Pull off the hairy "beards" and rinse again. Gently tap any open mussels and discard any that don't close.

Heat the oil in a wok over medium heat. Add the garlic and fry until crisp and golden. Now stir in the black bean sauce, ginger, rice wine, and soy sauce. Pour in the water and boil for 1 minute.

Throw in the mussels, cover, and simmer over medium heat for 3–4 minutes, until all the mussels have opened, discarding any that remain closed. Stir in the cilantro and serve immediately.

For jumbo shrimp with oyster sauce, heat the oil and add all the ingredients for the sauce, replacing the black bean sauce with oyster sauce. Omit the mussels and add 8 oz raw peeled jumbo shrimp. Simmer for 2–3 minutes, until pink all the way through and serve with a sprinkling of shredded scallions. **Calories per serving 105**

turkey ragout

Calories per serving **190**
Serves **4**
Preparation time **10 minutes**
Cooking time **1 hour**
  50 minutes

1 **turkey drumstick**, about
  1¼ lb
2 **garlic cloves**
15 **baby onions** or **shallots**
3 **carrots**, diagonally sliced
1¼ cups **red wine**
a few **thyme sprigs**
2 **bay leaves**
2 tablespoons chopped **flat-
  leaf parsley**
1 teaspoon **port wine jelly**
1 teaspoon **whole-grain
  mustard**
salt and **pepper**

Carefully remove the skin from the turkey drumstick and make a few cuts in the flesh. Finely slice 1 of the garlic cloves and push the slivers into the slashes. Crush the remaining garlic clove.

Transfer the drumstick to a large, flameproof casserole or roasting pan with the onions or shallots, carrots, crushed garlic, red wine, thyme, and bay leaves. Season well with salt and pepper, cover, and place in a preheated oven, 350°F, for about 1¾ hours or until the turkey is cooked through.

Remove the turkey and vegetables from the casserole and keep hot. Bring the sauce to a boil on the stove, discarding the bay leaves. Add the parsley, port wine jelly, and mustard. Boil for 5 minutes, until slightly thickened. Season with salt and pepper. Carve the turkey and serve with the juices in 4 serving bowls.

hot & sour soup

Calories per serving **161**
Serves **4**
Preparation time **10 minutes**
Cooking time **12 minutes**

3 cups **vegetable** or **fish stock**
4 dried **kaffir lime leaves**
1 inch piece **fresh ginger root**, peeled and grated
1 **red chile**, seeded and sliced
1 **lemon grass stalk**, lightly bruised
1½ cups sliced **mushrooms**
3½ oz **rice noodles**
2 cups **baby spinach**
4 oz cooked, peeled **jumbo shrimp**, or defrosted if frozen, rinsed with cold water and drained
2 tablespoons **lemon juice**
freshly ground **black pepper**

Put the stock, lime leaves, fresh ginger root, chile, and lemon grass in a large saucepan. Cover and bring to a boil. Add the mushrooms and simmer for 2 minutes. Break the noodles into short lengths, drop into the soup, and simmer for 3 minutes.

Add the baby spinach and shrimp and simmer for 2 minutes, until the shrimp are heated through. Add the lemon juice. Remove and discard the lemon grass stalk and season the soup with black pepper before serving.

For hot coconut soup, make up the soup as above, adding just 1¾ cups stock and 1 (12 oz) can coconut milk, plus 2 teaspoons prepared Thai red curry paste. Continue as above and serve sprinkled with a little chopped cilantro. **Calories per serving 348**

tuna & cranberry bean salad

Calories per serving **190**
Serves **4**
Preparation time **15 minutes,
    plus marinating**
Cooking time **3 minutes**

1 (14 oz) can **cranberry
    beans**, drained and rinsed
1 tablespoon **water** (optional)
2 tablespoons **extra virgin
    olive oil**
2 **garlic cloves**, crushed
1 **red chile**, seeded and finely
    chopped
2 **celery sticks**, thinly sliced
½ **red onion**, cut into thin
    wedges
1 (7 oz) can **tuna in olive oil**,
    drained and flaked
finely grated **zest** and **juice** of
    1 **lemon**
1¼ cups **wild arugula leaves**
salt and **pepper**

Heat the cranberry beans in a saucepan over medium heat for 3 minutes, adding the measured water if starting to stick to the bottom.

Put the oil, garlic, and chile in a large bowl. Stir in the celery, onion, and hot beans and season with salt and pepper. Cover and let marinate at room temperature for at least 30 minutes and up to 4 hours.

Stir in the tuna and lemon zest and juice. Gently toss in the arugula, taste and adjust the seasoning with extra salt, pepper, and lemon juice, if necessary.

For a mixed bean salad, heat the cranberry beans, as above, with 1 (15 oz) can drained and rinsed cannellini beans. Let marinate with the other salad ingredients as above, but also adding 2 tablespoons coarsely chopped flat-leaf parsley. After marinating, toss in 1¼ cups corn salad, season with salt and pepper, and serve. **Calories per serving 175**

bell pepper & feta rolls

Calories per serving **146 (not including arugula and crusty bread)**
Serves **4**
Preparation time **10 minutes, plus cooling**
Cooking time **10 minutes**

2 **red bell peppers**, cored, seeded, and quartered lengthwise
3½ oz **feta cheese**, thinly sliced or crumbled
16 **basil leaves**
16 **black ripe olives**, pitted and halved
2 tablespoons **pine nuts**, toasted
1 tablespoon **pesto**
1 tablespoon **fat-free French dressing**

Place the peppers skin side up on a baking sheet under a high broiler and cook for 7–8 minutes, until the skins are blackened. Remove the peppers and place them in a plastic bag. Fold over the top to seal and let cool for 20 minutes, then remove the skins.

Lay the skinned pepper quarters on a board and layer up the feta, basil leaves, olives, and pine nuts on each one.

Carefully roll up the peppers and secure with a toothpick. Place 2 pepper rolls on each serving plate.

Whisk together the pesto and French dressing in a small bowl and drizzle over the pepper rolls. Serve with arugula and crusty bread to mop up the juices, if desired.

For bell pepper, ricotta & sundried tomato rolls, broil and skin the peppers as above. Mix 5 chopped sundried tomatoes (the dry sort, not those in oil) into ½ cup ricotta cheese, also stirring in the basil and pine nuts. Omit the feta and black olives. Season with salt and pepper and use to top the pepper quarters. Roll up and serve as above. **Calories per serving 191**

chile shrimp with garlic & spinach

Calories per serving **124**
Serves **4**
Preparation time **10 minutes**
Cooking time **5 minutes**

2 tablespoons **vegetable oil**
1 **garlic clove**, sliced
1 **red Thai chile**, seeded and
  chopped
6 cups **baby spinach**
4 oz raw peeled **jumbo**
  shrimp
3 tablespoons **light soy sauce**
2 teaspoons **sugar**
1 tablespoon **Chinese rice**
  wine or **dry sherry**
1 tablespoon **Thai fish sauce**
  (nam pla)
6 tablespoons **water**
Chinese chive flowers or
  chives, to garnish

Heat the oil in a wok over high heat until the oil
starts to shimmer. Add the garlic and chile and stir-fry
for 30 seconds.

Add the spinach and shrimp and stir-fry in the oil for
1–2 minutes, until the spinach begins to wilt and the
shrimp are pink and cooked through.

Mix the soy sauce, sugar, rice wine, fish sauce, and
water together and add to the pan. Quickly stir-fry
together for another minute and serve while the
spinach still has texture. Garnish with Chinese chive
flowers or chives.

For angler fish with lime & spinach, replace the
shrimp with 8 oz angler fish cut into large chunks.
Stir-fry the fish with the garlic, chile and spinach as
above, adding in the grated zest and juice of 1 lime
with the soy sauce as you remove the stir-fry from
the heat. **Calories per serving 135**

shrimp & noodle soup

Calories per serving **161**
Serves **4**
Preparation time **10 minutes**
Cooking time **15 minutes**

3¾ cups **vegetable** or
　chicken stock
2 dried **kaffir lime leaves**
1 **lemon grass stalk**, lightly
　bruised
5 oz **dried egg noodles**
⅓ cup **frozen peas**
⅓ cup **frozen corn kernels**
3½ oz large **jumbo shrimp**,
　cooked, peeled, and
　deveined, or defrosted if
　frozen, rinsed with cold
　water, and drained
4 **scallions**, sliced
2 teaspoons **soy sauce**

Put the stock into a saucepan with the lime leaves and lemon grass, bring to a boil, then reduce the heat and simmer for 10 minutes.

Add the noodles to the stock and cook according to the package instructions. After 2 minutes, add the peas, corn, shrimp, scallions, and soy sauce and cook for 2 more minutes. Remove and discard the lemon grass. Serve the soup in warmed bowls.

For chicken & noodle soup, put the stock, lime leaves, and lemon grass into a saucepan, then add 2 boneless, skinless, chicken breasts that have been diced, bring to a boil, then simmer for 10 minutes. Continue as above. **Calories per serving 348**

piperade with pastrami

Calories per serving **186**
Serves **6**
Preparation time **20 minutes**
Cooking time **25 minutes**

6 large **eggs**
thyme sprigs, leaves removed,
   or large pinch of **dried**
   thyme, plus extra sprigs to
   garnish
1 tablespoon **olive oil**
4 oz **pastrami**, thinly sliced
salt and **pepper**

Sofrito
12 oz, or 3 small, **different**
   colored bell peppers
1 tablespoon **olive oil**
1 **onion**, finely chopped
2 **garlic cloves**, crushed
1 lb **tomatoes**, skinned,
   seeded, and chopped

Make the sofrito. Broil or cook the peppers directly in a gas flame for about 10 minutes, turning them until the skins have blistered and blackened. Rub the skins from the flesh and discard. Rinse the peppers under cold running water. Halve and seed and cut the flesh into strips.

Heat the oil in a large skillet, add the onion and cook gently for 10 minutes, until softened and transparent. Add the garlic, tomatoes, and peppers and simmer for 5 minutes, until any juice has evaporated from the tomatoes. Set aside until ready to serve.

Beat the eggs with the thyme and salt and pepper in a bowl. Reheat the sofrito. Heat the oil in a saucepan, add the eggs, stirring until they are lightly scrambled. Stir into the reheated sofrito and spoon onto plates.

Arrange slices of pastrami around the eggs and serve immediately, garnished with a little extra thyme.

For poached egg piperade, make the sofrito as above. Poach the 6 eggs instead of scrambling them. Meanwhile, split open 3 English muffins and toast on both sides. Divide the muffins among 6 plates, then spoon over the sofrito and sit the eggs over the muffins. Dust each egg with a tiny pinch of paprika and serve, omitting the pastrami. **Calories per serving 313**

scallops with lemon & ginger

Calories per serving **143**
Serves **4**
Preparation time **10 minutes**
Cooking time **10 minutes**

1 tablespoon **butter**
2 tablespoons **vegetable oil**
8 **scallops,** cut into thick slices
½ bunch of **scallions,** thinly
  sliced diagonally
½ teaspoon **ground turmeric**
3 tablespoons **lemon juice**
2 tablespoons **Chinese rice**
  wine or **dry sherry**
2 pieces **preserved stem**
  ginger with syrup, chopped
salt and **pepper**

Heat a wok until hot. Add the butter and 1 tablespoon
of the oil and heat over gentle heat until foaming.
Add the sliced scallops and stir-fry for 3 minutes, then
remove using a slotted spoon and set aside on a plate.

Return the wok to moderate heat, add the remaining
oil and heat until the oil starts to shimmer. Add the
scallions and turmeric and stir-fry for a few seconds.
Add the lemon juice and rice wine and bring to a boil,
then stir in the stem ginger.

Return the scallops and their juices to the wok and
toss until heated through. Season with salt and pepper
to taste and serve immediately.

For fennel & carrot salad, to serve with the scallops,
use a vegetable peeler to cut 1 fennel bulb and
2 carrots into thin shavings. Toss into a bowl with
a handful of cilantro leaves, the juice of ½ lemon,
and ½ teaspoon sesame oil. **Calories per serving 36**

chile & cilantro fish parcels

Calories per serving **127**
Serves **1**
Preparation time **15 minutes,
plus marinating and
chilling**
Cooking time **15 minutes**

4 oz **cod**, **coley**, or **haddock
tenderloin**
2 teaspoons **lemon juice**
1 tablespoon **fresh cilantro
leaves**
1 **garlic clove**
1 **green chile**, seeded and
chopped
¼ teaspoon **sugar**
2 teaspoons **plain yogurt**

Place the fish in a nonmetallic dish and sprinkle with the lemon juice. Cover and leave in the refrigerator to marinate for 15–20 minutes.

Put the cilantro, garlic, and chile in a food processor or blender and process until the mixture forms a paste. Add the sugar and yogurt and briefly process to blend.

Lay the fish on a sheet of foil. Coat the fish on both sides with the paste. Gather up the foil loosely and turn over at the top to seal. Return to the refrigerator for at least 1 hour.

Place the parcel on a baking sheet and bake in a preheated oven, 400°F, Gas Mark 6, for about 15 minutes, until the fish is just cooked.

For scallion & ginger fish parcels, place the fish tenderloin on a sheet of foil. Omit the above marinade. Combine 2 thinly sliced scallions and 1 teaspoon chopped ginger with a pinch of sugar and the juice and zest of ½ lime. Rub the mixture all over the fish, then seal and marinate the parcel as above for 30 minutes. Bake as above. **Calories per serving 106**

moroccan baked eggs

Calories per serving **170**
Serves **2**
Preparation time **10 minutes**
Cooking time **25–35 minutes**

½ tablespoon **olive oil**
½ **onion**, chopped
1 **garlic clove**, sliced
½ teaspoon **ras el hanout**
pinch of **ground cinnamon**
½ teaspoon **ground cilantro**
13 oz **cherry tomatoes**
2 tablespoons chopped
   cilantro leaves
2 **eggs**
salt and **pepper**

Heat the oil in a skillet over medium heat, add the onion and garlic and cook for 6–7 minutes or until softened and lightly golden, stirring occasionally. Stir in the spices and cook for another 1 minute. Add the tomatoes and season well with salt and pepper, then simmer gently for 8–10 minutes.

Sprinkle over 1 tablespoon of the cilantro, then divide the tomato mixture between 2 individual ovenproof dishes. Break an egg into each dish.

Bake in a preheated oven, 425°F, for 8–10 minutes, until the egg is set but the yolks are still slightly runny. Cook for 2–3 minutes more if you prefer the eggs to be cooked through. Serve sprinkled with the remaining cilantro.

caponata ratatouille

Calories per serving **90**
Serves **6**
Preparation time **20 minutes**
Cooking time **40 minutes**

1½ lb **eggplants**
1 large **onion**
1 tablespoon **olive oil**
3 **celery sticks**, coarsely
   chopped
a little **wine** (optional)
2 large **beef tomatoes**,
   skinned and seeded
1 teaspoon chopped **thyme**
¼–½ teaspoon **cayenne**
   pepper
2 tablespoons **capers**
handful of **pitted green olives**
¼ cup **white wine vinegar**
1 tablespoon **sugar**
1–2 tablespoons
   unsweetened cocoa
   powder (optional)
freshly ground **black pepper**

To garnish
toasted, chopped **almonds**
chopped **parsley**

Cut the eggplants and onion into ½ inch chunks.

Heat the oil in a nonstick skillet until very hot, add the eggplant, and fry for about 15 minutes, until very soft. Add a little boiling water to prevent sticking if necessary.

Meanwhile, place the onion and celery in a saucepan with a little water or wine. Cook for 5 minutes, until tender but still firm.

Add the tomatoes, thyme, cayenne pepper, and eggplant. Cook for 15 minutes, stirring occasionally. Add the capers, olives, wine vinegar, sugar, and cocoa powder (if using) and cook for 2–3 minutes.

Season with pepper and serve garnished with almonds and parsley. Serve hot or cold as a side dish, appetizer, or a main dish, with polenta and hot crusty bread, if desired.

For bell pepper & potato caponata, omit the eggplants, thyme, and cocoa powder. Broil and skin 2 red and 2 yellow bell peppers, following the method on page 32. Cook the onions and celery as above, then follow the remainder of the recipe, adding the skinned peppers and 1 lb cooked and halved new potatoes instead of the eggplants. **Calories per serving 169**

seafood with chiles

Calories per serving **174**

Serves **4**

Preparation time **5 minutes**

Cooking time **about 10 minutes**

1½ tablespoons **sunflower oil**

3–4 **garlic cloves**, finely chopped

1 **red bell pepper**, seeded and cut into bite-size pieces

1 **small onion**, cut into eighths

1 **carrot**, cut into matchsticks

14½ oz **prepared mixed seafood**, such as shrimp, squid, small scallops

1 inch piece of **fresh ginger root**, peeled and finely grated

2 tablespoons **vegetable** or **seafood stock** (see page 20)

1 tablespoon **oyster sauce**

½ tablespoon **light soy sauce**

1 **long red chile**, stemmed, seeded, and sliced diagonally

1–2 **scallions**, finely sliced

Heat the oil in a nonstick wok or skillet and stir-fry the garlic over medium heat until it is lightly browned.

Add the bell pepper, onion, and carrot and stir-fry for 2 minutes.

Add all the seafood together with the ginger, stock, oyster sauce, and soy sauce and stir-fry for 2–3 minutes or until the shrimp turn pink and all the seafood is cooked.

Add the chile and scallions and mix well together. Spoon onto a serving plate and serve immediately, with rice, if desired.

For seafood with pineapple sweet chile, stir-fry the bell pepper, onion, and carrot after the garlic has lightly browned. Add all the seafood, ginger, stock, oyster sauce, and 2–3 tablespoons pineapple-flavored sweet chili sauce (or plain if the flavored version is unavailable). Omit the scallions and add a handful of Thai basil leaves with the chile, lightly toss together for a minute to combine before serving. **Calories per serving 209**

vietnamese beef pho

Calories per serving **158**
Serves **6**
Preparation time **15 minutes**
Cooking time **about 45
minutes**

1 teaspoon **sunflower oil**
1 teaspoon **Szechuan
peppercorns**, coarsely
crushed
1 **lemon grass stalk**, sliced
1 **cinnamon stick**, broken into
pieces
2 **star anise**
1½ inch piece of **fresh ginger
root**, peeled, sliced
small bunch of **cilantro**
6 cups **beef stock**
1 tablespoon **fish sauce**
juice of **1 lime**
3½ oz **fine rice noodles**
8 oz **sirloin** or **minute beef
steak**, fat trimmed, meat
thinly sliced
1 cup **bean sprouts**, rinsed
4 **scallions**, thinly sliced
1 large **mild red chile**, thinly
sliced

Heat the oil in a saucepan, add the peppercorns, lemon grass, cinnamon, star anise, and ginger and cook for 1 minute to release their flavors. Cut the stems from the cilantro and add the stems to the pan with the stock. Bring to a boil, stirring, then cover and simmer for 40 minutes.

Strain the stock and return to the pan. Stir in the fish sauce and lime juice. Meanwhile, cook the noodles in a pan of boiling water as directed on the package, then drain and divide among 6 small bowls. Add the steak to the soup and cook for 1–2 minutes. Divide the bean sprouts, scallions, and chile among the bowls, then ladle the soup on top and finish with the remaining cilantro leaves, torn into pieces.

For Vietnamese shrimp soup, make up the flavored broth as above, using 6 cups chicken or vegetable stock and 2 kaffir lime leaves instead of the cinnamon. Simmer for 40 minutes, then drain and finish as above, adding 7 oz raw peeled shrimp and 2 cups sliced button mushrooms instead of the steak, cook for 4–5 minutes until the shrimp are pink. Finish with bean sprouts, scallions, and chile as above. **Calories per serving 135**

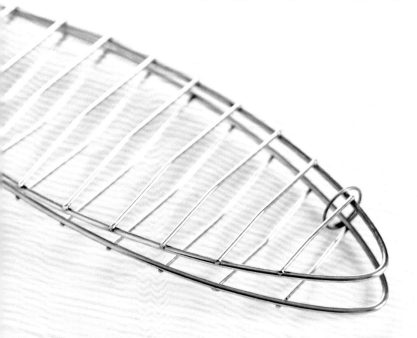

recipes
under 300
calories

seafood & vegetable stir-fry

Calories per serving **220**
Serves **4**
Preparation time **18 minutes**
Cooking time **10 minutes**

8 oz **live mussels**
1 ⅓ cups peeled and thickly
   sliced **water chestnuts**
1 tablespoon **sugar**
½ teaspoon **black pepper**
2 tablespoons **vegetable oil**
1 **sweet white onion**, sliced
4 oz raw peeled **jumbo**
   shrimp
4 **scallions**, trimmed and
   diagonally sliced
½ teaspoon **dried red pepper**
   flakes, plus extra to garnish
1 cup **sugar snap peas**,
   trimmed and diagonally
   halved
1 cup **bean sprouts**
3 tablespoons **light soy sauce**
2 tablespoons **yellow bean**
   sauce
2 tablespoons **Chinese rice**
   wine or **dry sherry**
chervil sprigs, to garnish

Scrub the mussels thoroughly under cold running water. Pull off the hairy "beards" and rinse again. Gently tap any open mussels and discard any that do not close.

Sprinkle the water chestnuts with the sugar and pepper and set aside.

Heat the oil in a wok over high heat until the oil starts to shimmer. Add the onion and mussels and stir-fry quickly for 1 minute. Put a lid on the wok and cook for 3–4 minutes or until the mussels have opened. Discard any mussels that remain closed.

Add the water chestnuts, shrimp, scallions, red pepper flakes, sugar snaps, and bean sprouts to the wok and stir-fry for 1–2 minutes or until the shrimp have turned pink and are cooked through.

Mix together the soy sauce, yellow bean sauce, and rice wine and pour over the ingredients in the wok. Stir-fry for another 1–2 minutes until hot. Garnish with red pepper flakes and chervil sprigs. Serve with rice, if desired.

For quick mixed seafood stir-fry, replace the live mussels and raw shrimp with 8 oz mixed cooked seafood, now available in many supermarkets. Cook the onions as above, then add the mixed seafood to the wok at the same time as the sauce ingredients. Complete the recipe as above. **Calories per serving 232**

minestrone

Calories per serving **260**
Serves **4**
Preparation time **5 minutes**
Cooking time **23 minutes**

2 tablespoons **olive oil**
1 **onion**, chopped
1 **garlic clove**, crushed
2 **celery sticks**, chopped
1 **leek**, finely sliced
1 **carrot**, chopped
1 (14½ oz) can **diced
  tomatoes**
2½ cups **chicken** or
  vegetable stock
1 **zucchini**, diced
½ small **cabbage**, shredded
1 **bay leaf**
⅓ cup **canned white kidney
  beans**
3 oz **dried spaghetti**, broken
  into small pieces, or small
  pasta shapes
1 tablespoon chopped
flat-leaf parsley
salt and **pepper**
grated **Parmesan cheese**, to
  serve

Heat the oil in a large saucepan. Add the onion, garlic, celery, leek, and carrot and cook over medium heat, stirring occasionally, for 5 minutes. Add the tomatoes, stock, zucchini, cabbage, bay leaf, and kidney beans. Bring to a boil, lower the heat, and simmer for 10 minutes.

Add the pasta and season with salt and pepper to taste. Stir well and cook for another 8 minutes. Keep stirring because the soup may stick to the bottom of the pan. Just before serving, add the parsley and stir well. Ladle into individual bowls and serve with grated Parmesan.

For minestrone with arugula & basil pesto, make up the soup as above, then ladle into bowls. Top with spoonfuls of pesto made by finely chopping ½ cup arugula leaves and 1 cup basil leaves, 1 garlic clove, and 3 tablespoons pine nuts. Mix with 2 tablespoons freshly grated Parmesan, a little salt and pepper, and ¼ cup olive oil. Alternatively, put all the pesto ingredients into a blender or food processor and blend together. (Use only half the quantity the recipe makes to maintain the 350 calorie serving.) **Calories per serving 350**

beef in black bean sauce

Calories per serving **294**
Serves **4**
Preparation time **10 minutes**
Cooking time **10 minutes**

3 tablespoons **peanut oil**
1 lb **lean beef**, cut into thin
 slices
1 **red bell pepper**, cored,
 seeded, and cut into strips
6 **baby corn ears**, cut in half
 lengthwise
1 **green chile**, seeded and cut
 into strips
3 **shallots**, cut into thin
 wedges
2 tablespoons **black bean
 sauce**
¼ cup **water**
1 teaspoon **cornstarch** mixed
 to a paste with 1 tablespoon
 water
salt

Heat 1 tablespoon of the oil in a wok over high heat
until the oil starts to shimmer. Add half the beef, season
with salt, and stir-fry for 2 minutes. When it begins to
brown, lift the beef onto a plate using a slotted spoon.
Heat another 1 tablespoon of the oil and stir-fry the
rest of the beef in the same way.

Return the wok to the heat and wipe it clean with paper
towels. Heat the remaining oil and add the bell pepper,
corn, chile, and shallots. Stir-fry for 2 minutes before
adding the black bean sauce, the measured water, and
the cornstarch paste. Bring to a boil, return the beef to
the wok, and stir-fry until the sauce thickens and coats
the stir-fry in a velvety glaze. Serve with rice, if desired.

For jumbo shrimp with scallions & black bean
sauce, replace the beef with 8 oz raw peeled jumbo
shrimp. Replace the corn, green chile, and shallots with
¾ cup bean sprouts, 1 red chile, and 3 scallions cut
into ½ inch pieces, and cook as above. **Calories per
serving 171**

pork with broccoli & mushrooms

Calories per serving **286**

Serves **4**

Preparation time **10 minutes**

Cooking time **10 minutes**

1 tablespoon **sesame seeds**

3 tablespoons **peanut oil**

13 oz **lean pork**, sliced into thin strips

1 cup small **broccoli** florets

5 oz **shiitake mushrooms**, trimmed and halved, if large

3 **baby leeks**, trimmed, cleaned, and thinly sliced

3 tablespoons **Chinese rice wine** or **dry sherry**

3 tablespoons **oyster sauce**

2 tablespoons **malt vinegar**

1 teaspoon **sugar**

1 teaspoon **honey**

½ teaspoon **sesame oil**

1 **red chile**, thinly sliced

Fry the sesame seeds in a dry wok over medium heat, stirring until golden. Set aside.

Heat half the oil in a wok over high heat until the oil starts to shimmer. Add half the pork and stir-fry for 2 minutes until golden. Remove the pork using a slotted spoon and set aside. Heat the remaining oil and stir-fry the rest of the pork in the same way, then return the first batch of pork to the wok.

Add the broccoli, mushrooms, and leeks and stir-fry for 2 minutes. Add the rice wine, oyster sauce, malt vinegar, sugar, and honey and cook for 1 more minute. Remove from the heat, stir in the toasted sesame seeds, sesame oil, and chile, and serve.

For scallion rice, to serve with the pork, heat 1 tablespoon peanut oil in a wok over high heat. Add 4 sliced scallions and give them a quick stir, then add 2 cups cold cooked rice. Stir until heated through, then add ½ teaspoon sesame oil and 1 tablespoon light soy sauce. Stir well and serve. **Calories per serving 124**

warm scallop salad

Calories per serving **257**
Serves **4**
Preparation time **10 minutes**
Cooking time **3 minutes**

8 oz **wild strawberries**, hulled
2 tablespoons **balsamic
    vinegar**
1 tablespoon **lemon juice**,
    plus juice of **1 lemon**
3 tablespoons **olive oil**
12 **scallops**, without corals,
    cut into 3 slices
6 cups **mixed salad greens**
salt and **black pepper**

To garnish
1 tablespoon **olive oil**
3 **leeks**, cut into matchstick-
    thin strips
20 **wild strawberries** or
    8 **larger strawberries**, sliced

Put the strawberries, vinegar, 1 tablespoon lemon juice, and oil in a food processor or blender and process until smooth. Pass through a fine-mesh strainer or cheesecloth to remove the seeds and set aside.

Season the scallops with salt and pepper and the remaining lemon juice.

Prepare the garnish. Heat the oil in a nonstick skillet, add the leeks, and cook over high heat, stirring, for 1 minute, or until golden brown. Remove and set aside.

Add the scallop slices to the pan and cook for 20–30 seconds on each side. Divide the salad greens into quarters and pile in the center of individual serving plates. Arrange the scallop slices over the salad.

Heat the strawberry mixture gently in a small saucepan for 20–30 seconds, then pour over the scallops and salad greens. Sprinkle with the leeks and garnish with the strawberries. Sprinkle with a little pepper and serve.

For scallops with soy & honey dressing, whisk together 2 tablespoons extra virgin olive oil, 1 teaspoon sesame oil, 1 tablespoon light soy sauce, 2 teaspoons balsamic vinegar, 1 teaspoon honey, and black pepper to taste in a bowl. Cook the scallops as above (omitting the leeks) and arrange over the salad. Heat the dressing gently as above, then pour over the scallops and salad greens. **Calories per serving 173**

bean, kabanos & bell pepper

Calories per serving **250 (not including walnut bread)**

Serves **4**

Preparation time **10 minutes, plus cooling**

Cooking time **20 minutes**

3 **red bell peppers**, cored and seeded

1 tablespoon **olive oil**

1 **onion**, sliced

3 oz **kabanos sausage**, thinly sliced

2 (15 oz) cans **butter** or **lima beans**, rinsed and drained

1 tablespoon **balsamic vinegar**

1 **red chile**, seeded and sliced

2 tablespoons chopped **fresh cilantro**

Put the peppers on a baking sheet, skin side up, and cook under a preheated hot broiler for 8–10 minutes until the skins are blackened. Cover with damp paper towels. When the peppers are cool enough to handle, remove the skins and slice the flesh.

Heat the oil in a nonstick skillet, add the onion, and fry for 5–6 minutes, until soft. Add the kabanos sausage and fry for 1–2 minutes, until crisp.

Mix together the beans and balsamic vinegar, then add the onion and kabanos mixture and the peppers and chile. Serve the salad with walnut bread, if desired.

For bean, bell pepper & olive salad with haloumi,

omit the kabanos sausage and mix 1/3 cup halved pitted black ripe olives with the beans. Slice and broil 3 oz haloumi. Divide the salad among bowls and top with the haloumi. **Calories per serving 248**

steamed fish with preserved plums

Calories per serving **259**
Serves **4**
Preparation time **30 minutes**
Cooking time **20 minutes**

2 lb **whole fish** (such as
  pomfret, flounder, snapper,
  or sea bass), cleaned, scaled
  (if necessary), gutted, scored
  3–4 times with a sharp knife
1½ inch piece of **fresh ginger
  root**, peeled, finely shredded
¾ cup thinly sliced **button
  mushrooms**
2 oz **smoked bacon**, cut into
  thin strips
4 **scallions**, cut into 1 inch
  lengths
2 small **preserved plums**,
  lightly bruised
2 tablespoons **light soy sauce**
pinch of **ground white pepper**

To garnish
cilantro leaves
a few slices of **red chile**

Place the fish on a deep plate slightly larger than the
fish. Use a plate that will fit on the rack of a traditional
bamboo steamer basket or on a steamer rack inside a
wok. Sprinkle the fish with the ginger, mushrooms, bacon,
scallions, preserved plums, soy sauce, and pepper.

Fill a wok or steamer pan with water, cover and bring to
a rolling boil on high heat. Set the rack or basket over
the boiling water. Cover and steam for 15–20 minutes
(depending on the variety and size of the fish) or until
the tip of a sharp knife will slide easily into the fish.

Remove the fish from the steamer and place on a
warm serving plate. Garnish with cilantro leaves and
chile slices, and serve with jasmine rice, if desired.

For steamed fish with ginger & scallions, omit
the mushrooms, smoked bacon, and preserved plums.
Add 1 tablespoon sunflower oil and 1 tablespoon
sesame oil, and increase the amount of light soy sauce
to 2–3 tablespoons. Drizzle these on top of the fish
with the ginger and scallions, and steam as above.
Calories per serving 263

italian broccoli & egg salad

Calories per serving **203**
Serves **4**
Preparation time **10 minutes**
Cooking time **8 minutes**

10 oz **broccoli**
2 small **leeks**, about 10 oz in
  total, trimmed, slit, and well
  rinsed
¼ cup **lemon juice**
2 tablespoons **olive oil**
2 teaspoons **honey**
1 tablespoon **capers**, well
  drained
2 tablespoons chopped
  tarragon, plus extra sprigs
  to garnish
4 hard-cooked **eggs**
salt and **pepper**

Cut the broccoli into florets and thickly slice the stems
and the leeks. Put the broccoli in the top of a steamer,
cook for 3 minutes, add the leeks and cook for another
2 minutes.

Mix together the lemon juice, oil, honey, capers, and
tarragon in a salad bowl and season to taste.

Shell and roughly chop the eggs.

Add the broccoli and leeks to the dressing, toss
together and sprinkle with the chopped eggs. Garnish
with tarragon sprigs and serve warm with extra thickly
sliced whole-wheat bread, if desired.

For broccoli, cauliflower & egg salad, use 5 oz
broccoli and 5 oz cauliflower instead of 10 oz broccoli.
Cut the cauliflower into small florets and steam with
the broccoli. Serve with a blue cheese dressing made
by mixing together 3 oz blue cheese, 6 chopped
sundried tomatoes, and 3 tablespoons balsamic vinegar.
Calories per serving 312

baked cod with tomatoes & olives

Calories per serving **239**
Serves **4**
Preparation time **5 minutes**
Cooking time **15 minutes**

1 cup **cherry tomatoes**,
   halved
½ cup **pitted black ripe olives**
2 tablespoons **capers**
4 **thyme** sprigs, plus extra to
   garnish
4 **cod tenderloins**, about 6
   oz each
2 tablespoons **extra virgin
   olive oil**
2 tablespoons **balsamic
   vinegar**
salt and **black pepper**

Combine the tomatoes, olives, capers, and thyme sprigs in a roasting pan. Nestle the cod tenderloins in the pan, drizzle over the oil and balsamic vinegar and season to taste with salt and pepper.

Bake in a preheated oven, 400°F, for 15 minutes.

Transfer the fish, tomatoes, and olives to warmed plates. Spoon the pan juices over the fish. Serve immediately with a mixed green salad, if desired.

For steamed cod with lemon, arrange a cod tenderloin on each of 4 x 12 inch squares of foil. Top each with ½ teaspoon grated lemon zest, a squeeze of lemon juice, 1 tablespoon extra virgin olive oil, and salt and pepper to taste. Fold the edges of the foil together to form parcels, transfer to a baking sheet, and cook in a preheated oven, 400°F, for 15 minutes. Remove and let rest for 5 minutes. Open the parcels and serve sprinkled with chopped parsley. **Calories per serving 253**

pork with savoy cabbage

Calories per serving **227**
Serves **4**
Preparation time **15 minutes**
Cooking time **40 minutes**

1 tablespoon **sesame seeds**
2 **garlic cloves**, very finely
   sliced
3 **scallions**, diagonally sliced
   into ¾ inch pieces
½ teaspoon **cayenne pepper**
10 oz **pork loin**, cut into thick
   strips
2 tablespoons **olive oil**
2 teaspoons **sesame oil**
2 tablespoons **soy sauce**
2 teaspoons **honey**
4 cups shredded **Savoy
   cabbage**

Heat a dry heavy skillet until hot, add the sesame seeds, and cook, shaking constantly, for 1–2 minutes, until golden brown and aromatic. Remove to a cool plate and set aside.

Combine the garlic, scallions, and cayenne pepper in a bowl. Add the pork and mix well.

Heat the oils in a skillet, add the pork in 3 batches, and stir-fry over high heat for 5 minutes on each side, or until golden and cooked through. Remove from the pan with a slotted spoon.

Add the soy sauce, honey, and cabbage to the pan and toss to mix. Cover and cook over a medium heat for 5–6 minutes.

Return the pork to the pan, add the sesame seeds and toss well. Serve immediately.

For orange & mustard seed rice to serve with the pork, put 1 cup jasmine rice in a saucepan and add 1¾ cups cold water and ½ teaspoon salt. Bring to a boil, then reduce the heat, cover with a tight-fitting lid and simmer over very low heat for 12 minutes. Meanwhile, melt 2 teaspoons butter in a small saucepan, add 1 tablespoon mustard seeds and grated zest of 1 orange and cook gently, stirring, for 2–3 minutes, until the mustard seeds turn golden. Remove the rice from the heat, pour in the mustard seed mixture and replace the lid. Let stand for 10 minutes, then stir well and serve. **Calories per serving 269**

smoked salmon cones

Calories per serving **270**
Serves **4**
Preparation time **15 minutes**

2 **small cucumbers,** halved
    lengthwise, seeded, and cut
    into thin strips
1 teaspoon prepared **English
    mustard**
1 tablespoon **white wine
    vinegar**
½ teaspoon **sugar**
1 tablespoon finely chopped
    dill weed
2 **flour tortillas**
¼ cup **crème fraîche** or **sour
    cream**
4 oz **smoked salmon
    trimmings,** any larger pieces
    cut into wide strips
salt and **pepper**

Put the cucumber strips in a shallow glass or ceramic bowl. In a small bowl, mix together the mustard, vinegar, sugar, and dill. Season well with salt and pepper, then pour over the cucumbers. Let stand for 5 minutes.

Cut the tortillas in half and lay on a board or work surface. Spread 1 tablespoon crème fraîche over each tortilla half.

Divide the smoked salmon pieces between the tortillas and top with the cucumber mixture. Add a little salt and pepper, if desired, and roll up each tortilla to form a cone around the filling. Secure each cone with a toothpick, if desired.

For chicken & mango cones, put 4 oz diced, cooked chicken breast meat, 1 large peeled, pitted, and diced mango, and 1 tablespoon chopped cilantro leaves in a bowl. Add ¼ cup mayonnaise, a squeeze of lime juice, and salt and pepper to taste. Toss gently to combine, then divide among the tortilla halves and roll up, as above. **Calories per serving 310**

duck, pear & pomegranate salad

Calories per serving **276 (not including molasses)**

Serves **4**

Preparation time **15 minutes**

Cooking time **15–20 minutes**

2 large, lean **duck breasts**

2 **Comice pears**, cored and diced

3 cups **mixed herb and salad greens**

1/3 cup **walnut pieces**

seeds from 1 **pomegranate**

Dressing

2 teaspoons **lime juice**

2 teaspoons **raspberry vinegar**

2 teaspoons **pomegranate molasses** (optional—see right for homemade)

2 tablespoons **walnut oil**

salt and **pepper**

Remove any excess fat from the duck breasts and score the surface using a sharp knife. Heat a ridged grill pan until hot, then add the duck breasts, skin side down, and cook for 8–10 minutes. Turn them over and cook for another 5–10 minutes or until cooked to the pinkness desired. Remove from the pan, cover with foil, and let rest.

Mix together the pears and mixed salad in a bowl. Arrange on serving plates and sprinkle with the walnut pieces.

Whisk together all the dressing ingredients in a bowl and season with salt and pepper to taste. Drizzle over the salad.

Slice the duck breasts and arrange on the salad. Sprinkle with the pomegranate seeds and serve immediately.

For homemade pomegranate molasses, juice 2 large pomegranates with a citrus press or remove the seeds and pulse in a food processor or blender. Pour the juice into a small saucepan, add 1 tablespoon sugar and stir until the sugar dissolves. Bring to a boil, then reduce the heat and simmer rapidly until reduced to a thick, sticky molasses. Cool and store in an airtight bottle in the refrigerator for up to 2 weeks. **Calories per serving 319**

white bean soup provençal

Calories per serving **200 (not including crusty bread)**
Serves **6**
Preparation time **15 minutes, plus soaking**
Cooking time **1¼–1¾ hours**

3 tablespoons **olive oil**
2 **garlic cloves**, crushed
1 small **red bell pepper**, cored, seeded, and chopped
1 **onion**, finely chopped
8 oz **tomatoes**, finely chopped
1 teaspoon finely chopped **thyme**
2 cups **dried white kidney** or **cannellini beans**, soaked overnight in cold water, rinsed, and drained
2½ cups **water**
2½ cups **vegetable stock**
2 tablespoons finely chopped **flat-leaf parsley**
salt and **pepper**

Heat the oil in a large heavy saucepan, add the garlic, red pepper, and onion and cook over medium heat for 5 minutes or until softened.

Add the tomatoes and thyme and cook for 1 minute. Add the beans and pour in the measured water and stock. Bring to a boil, then reduce the heat, cover, and simmer for 1–1½ hours, until the beans are tender (you may need to allow for a longer cooking time, depending on how old the beans are).

Sprinkle in the parsley and season with salt and pepper. Serve immediately in warm soup bowls with fresh, crusty bread.

For Spanish white bean soup, add 3½ oz diced chorizo sausage when frying the onions, garlic, and red pepper. Stir in 1 teaspoon pimentón (Spanish smoked paprika) or 1 teaspoon mild chili powder. Cook for 1 minute, until fragrant, then add the tomatoes and continue the recipe as above.
Calories per serving 325

sweet & sour angler fish & shrimp

Calories per serving **217**
Serves **4**
Preparation time **10 minutes**
Cooking time **7 minutes**

10 oz **angler fish tail**, cut into chunks

7 oz raw peeled **jumbo shrimp**

2 tablespoons **peanut oil**

1 inch piece of **fresh ginger root**, peeled and finely grated

7 oz **carrots**, cut into matchsticks

7 oz **sugar snap peas**, halved

4 **scallions**, thinly sliced

salt and **black pepper**

Sweet and sour sauce
²/₃ cup **fish** or **vegetable stock**

2½ tablespoons **light soy sauce**

2 teaspoons **tomato paste**

1 tablespoon **cider vinegar**

2 teaspoons **sugar**

2 teaspoons **cornstarch**

½ teaspoon **salt**

Combine all the ingredients for the sauce. Season the angler fish and shrimp with salt and pepper.

Heat the oil in a wok over high heat until the oil starts to shimmer. Add the fish and shrimp and cook for 2 minutes, carefully turning the fish occasionally, then add the ginger, carrots, sugar snaps, and scallions.

Fry for 30 seconds, then add the sauce and bring to a boil. Turn down the heat and simmer for 2–3 minutes until the vegetables are just tender and the fish is cooked through. Serve immediately.

For aromatic angler fish & shrimp, cook the fish as above up to the stage where you would have added the sweet and sour sauce. Omit this and instead stir-fry for another 2 minutes, then remove from the heat and toss in a handful each of torn cilantro and mint and the juice of 1 lime. **Calories per serving 185**

butternut squash & ricotta frittata

Calories per serving **248**
Serves **6**
Preparation time **10 minutes**
Cooking time **25–30 minutes**

1 tablespoon **extra virgin
    canola oil**
1 **red onion**, thinly sliced
2 cups diced **butternut
    squash**
8 **eggs**
1 tablespoon chopped **thyme**
2 tablespoons chopped **sage**
½ cup **ricotta cheese**
salt and **pepper**

Heat the oil in a large, deep skillet with an ovenproof handle over medium-low heat, add the onion and butternut squash, then cover loosely and cook gently, stirring frequently, for 18–20 minutes or until softened and golden.

Lightly beat the eggs, thyme, sage, and ricotta in a small bowl, then season well with salt and pepper and pour over the butternut squash.

Cook for another 2–3 minutes until the egg is almost set, stirring occasionally with a heat-resistant rubber spatula to prevent the base from burning.

Slide the pan under a preheated broiler, keeping the handle away from the heat, and broil for 3–4 minutes or until the egg is set and the frittata is golden. Slice into 6 wedges and serve hot.

beef & barley brö

Calories per serving **209**
Serves **6**
Preparation time **20 minutes**
Cooking time **2 hours**

2 tablespoons **butter**
8 oz **braising beef**, fat
  trimmed away and meat cut
  into small cubes
1 large **onion**, finely chopped
1 cup diced **rutabaga**
¾ cup diced **carrot**
½ cup **pearl barley**
2 quarts **beef stock**
2 teaspoons **dry English
  mustard** (optional)
salt and **pepper**
chopped **parsley**, to garnish

Heat the butter in a large saucepan, add the beef and onion and sauté for 5 minutes, stirring, until the beef is browned and the onion just beginning to color.

Stir in the diced vegetables, pearl barley, stock, and mustard, if using. Season with salt and pepper and bring to a boil. Cover and simmer for 1¾ hours, stirring occasionally, until the meat and vegetables are very tender. Taste and adjust the seasoning if needed. Ladle the soup into bowls and sprinkle with a little chopped parsley.

For lamb & barley hotchpot, substitute the beef with 8 oz diced lamb tenderloin and fry with the onion as above. Add the sliced white part of 1 leek, 1 cup each of diced rutabaga, carrot, and potato, then mix in ¼ cup pearl barley, 2 quarts lamb stock, 2–3 sprigs of rosemary, and salt and pepper. Bring to a boil, then cover and simmer for 1¾ hours. Discard the rosemary, add the remaining thinly sliced green leek, and cook for 10 minutes. Ladle into bowls and sprinkle with a little extra chopped rosemary to serve. **Calories per serving 209**

baked fish with lemon grass

Calories per serving **284**
Serves **4**
Preparation time **10 minutes**
Cooking time **20–25 minutes**

2 lb **whole fish** (such as
    mackerel, St Peter fish,
    sea bream, red snapper, or
    mullet), cleaned and scaled
    (if necessary), gutted, scored
    3–4 times with a sharp knife
4 x 5 inch stalks **lemon grass**,
    cut diagonally into 1 inch
    lengths
2 **carrots**, cut into matchsticks
¼ cup **light soy sauce**
2 tablespoons **lime juice**
1 **red chile**, finely chopped

To garnish
cilantro leaves
a few slices of **red chile**
a few slices of **lemon**, to serve

Place the fish in a baking dish and sprinkle with the lemon grass, carrots, 1½ tablespoons of the light soy sauce, and the lime juice.

Cover the baking dish with foil and bake in a preheated oven, 350°F, for 20–25 minutes or until the tip of a sharp knife will slide easily into the flesh and come out clean. Place the fish on a warm serving plate and spoon over the sauce. Garnish with cilantro leaves and chile and serve with the lemon slices.

Spoon the remaining light soy sauce into a small bowl with the chile and serve separately.

Serve with other dishes, with boiled rice, or on its own as a light meal with stir-fried or steamed vegetables.

For cod tenderloins with lemon grass, replace the whole fish with 4 x 8 oz cod tenderloins, removing any fine bones. Sprinkle as above and bake for 15–17 minutes or until the fish is cooked. Garnish with finely chopped red chile and serve as above. **Calories per serving 268**

tuna steaks with wasabi dressing

Calories per serving **279**
Serves **4**
Preparation time **5 minutes**
Cooking time **6–7 minutes**

4 **tuna steaks**, about 5 oz
  each
2 teaspoons **mixed
  peppercorns**, crushed
2½ cups **sugar snap peas**
1 teaspoon **toasted sesame
  oil**
2 teaspoons **sesame seeds**,
  lightly toasted

Dressing
2 tablespoons **light soy sauce**
¼ cup **mirin**
1 teaspoon **sugar**
1 teaspoon **wasabi paste**

Season the tuna steaks with the crushed peppercorns.
Heat a ridged grill pan over medium-high heat and grill the
tuna steaks for 2 minutes on each side until browned but
still pink in the center. Remove from the pan and let rest.

Put the sugar snap peas in a steamer basket and lower
into a shallow saucepan of boiling water so that the
peas are not quite touching the water. Drizzle with the
sesame oil, cover, and steam for 2–3 minutes or until
tender. Alternatively, cook the peas in a bamboo or
electric steamer.

Place all of the dressing ingredients in a screw-top jar
and seal with a tight-fitting lid. Shake vigorously until
well combined.

Divide the sugar snap peas among 4 serving dishes,
then cut the tuna steaks in half diagonally and arrange
over the peas. Drizzle with the prepared dressing and
sprinkle with the sesame seeds. Serve immediately,
with cellophane rice noodles, if desired.

For tuna carpaccio, roll 1 lb tuna tenderloin in the
peppercorns and seal on all sides in a very hot skillet.
Cool, wrap in plastic wrap, and place in the freezer for
1 hour until semi-frozen. Remove and cut into very
thin slices. Arrange the slices on large plates and
drizzle with the dressing. Serve with the steamed and
chilled sugar snap peas, sprinkled with sesame seeds.
Calories per serving 245

thai-style beef salad

Calories per serving **253**
Serves **4**
Preparation time **20 minutes**
Cooking time **10 minutes**

4 oz **green papaya**, peeled
and seeded
4 oz **green mango**, peeled
and pitted
handful of **mint leaves**,
chopped
handful of **Thai basil leaves**
2 small, elongated **shallots**,
finely sliced
1 tablespoon **vegetable oil**
4 **sirloin steaks**, about 4 oz
each

Dressing
½ inch piece of **fresh ginger
root**, peeled and finely sliced
1½ tablespoons **palm sugar**
or packed **light brown sugar**
½ **red chile**, seeded and finely
sliced
juice of 2 **limes**
2 tablespoons **Thai fish sauce**

Grate or slice the papaya and mango into long, thin strips. Put the papaya and mango, mint and basil leaves in a large salad bowl and mix together, then stir in the shallots.

Make the dressing. Crush the ginger and sugar using a mortar and pestle. Add the chile, lime juice, and fish sauce, to taste.

Heat a ridged grill pan over high heat, add the oil, and fry the steaks for 5 minutes on each side or until cooked to the pinkness desired. Remove from the pan and let rest for 5 minutes.

Slice the steaks diagonally into thin slices and arrange on serving plates. Add the dressing to the salad, mix well to combine, and serve with the steak.

For toasted rice khao koor, a special garnish you can add to this salad, put 3 tablespoons raw jasmine rice in a small skillet over medium heat, stirring continuously, until all the rice is golden in color. Let the rice cool, then grind it coarsely in a spice grinder or using a mortar and pestle, and sprinkle over the finished salad. **Calories per serving 42**

steamed citrus sea bass

Calories per serving **256**
Serves **4**
Preparation time **15 minutes**
Cooking time **20 minutes**

1 whole **sea bream** or **sea
   bass**, about 1 lb 10 oz–2 lb,
   scaled and gutted
3 tablespoons **chicken stock**
   or **water**
3 tablespoons **Chinese rice
   wine** or **dry sherry**
peel of 1 small **orange**, thinly
   sliced
1 inch piece **fresh ginger
   root**, thinly sliced
1 teaspoon **sugar**
3 tablespoons **light soy sauce**
½ teaspoon **sesame oil**
1 **garlic clove**, thinly sliced
3 **scallions**, thinly sliced
1 tablespoon **peanut oil**

Score 3 diagonal slits along each side of the fish with
a sharp knife, then cut in the opposite direction to make
a diamond pattern.

Cut 2 large pieces of foil about 1½ times the length of
the fish. Place the fish in the center of the double layer
of foil and lift it up around the fish slightly. Pour the
stock and rice wine over the fish, then sprinkle with
the orange peel and half the ginger.

Place a circular rack inside a wok and pour in enough
water to come just below the top of the rack. Place the
lid on the wok and bring the water to a rolling boil.
Carefully sit the open fish parcel on the rack, cover
with the lid, and steam for 15–18 minutes, until the
flesh inside the slits is opaque. Carefully remove the
fish from the wok and place on a serving dish.

Stir the sugar into a bowl with the soy sauce and
sesame oil, then pour the liquid over the fish with the
garlic, scallions, and remaining ginger.

Heat the peanut oil in a small skillet over high heat
until smoking hot, then pour it over the fish. This will
crisp up the scallions and ginger and release their
aroma. Serve immediately.

**For steamed sea bream with mushrooms &
tomatoes**, place the fish on the foil as above and
season with salt and pepper. Top with 2 tablespoons
olive oil, ½ cup dry white wine, 3 oz trimmed and sliced
shiitake mushrooms, and 6 halved cherry tomatoes.
Steam in the wok as above. **Calories per serving 292**

spring minestrone

Calories per serving **221**
Serves **4**
Preparation time **15 minutes**
Cooking time **55 minutes**

2 tablespoons **olive oil**
1 **onion**, thinly sliced
2 **carrots**, peeled and diced
2 **celery sticks**, diced
2 **garlic cloves**, peeled
1 **potato**, peeled and diced
²/₃ cup **peas** or **fava beans**,
   thawed if frozen
1 **zucchini**, diced
1 cup **green beans**, trimmed
   and cut into 1½ inch pieces
4 oz **plum tomatoes**, skinned
   and chopped
5 cups **vegetable stock**
3 oz **small pasta shapes**
10 **basil leaves**, torn
salt and **pepper**

To serve
olive oil
grated **Parmesan cheese**

Heat the oil in a large, heavy saucepan over low heat, add the onion, carrots, celery, and garlic and cook, stirring occasionally, for 10 minutes. Add the potato, peas or fava beans, zucchini, and green beans and cook, stirring frequently, for 2 minutes. Add the tomatoes, season with salt and pepper, and cook for another 2 minutes.

Pour in the stock and bring to a boil, then reduce the heat and simmer gently for 20 minutes or until all the vegetables are very tender.

Add the pasta and basil to the soup and cook, stirring frequently, until the pasta is al dente. Season with salt and pepper to taste.

Ladle into bowls, drizzle with olive oil, and sprinkle with Parmesan. Serve with toasted country bread, if desired, or Parmesan toasts (see below).

For Parmesan toasts, to serve as an accompaniment, toast 4–6 slices of ciabatta on one side only under a preheated medium broiler. Brush the other side with 2–3 tablespoons olive oil and sprinkle with dried red pepper flakes and 2 tablespoons grated Parmesan cheese, then cook under the preheated broiler until golden and crisp. **Calories per serving 185**

flounder with herbed coconut crust

Calories per serving **201**
Serves **4**
Preparation time **5 minutes**
Cooking time **15 minutes**

⅓ cup **shredded coconut**
1 cup **bread crumbs**
2 tablespoons chopped
chives
pinch of **paprika**
4 **skinless flounder
tenderloins**
salt and **pepper**
lime wedges, to serve

Mix together the coconut, bread crumbs, chives, and paprika and season with salt and pepper to taste.

Arrange the fish tenderloins on a baking sheet, top each one with some of the coconut mixture and cook in a preheated oven, 350°F, for 15 minutes.

Serve the fish with lime wedges and accompanied with baked potatoes and an arugula salad, if desired.

For lemon sole with an almond crust, substitute the flounder tenderloins with 4 skinless lemon sole tenderloins. In the topping, use ½ cup sliced almonds instead of coconut. Serve the fish with new potatoes, watercress, and lemon wedges.
Calories per serving 232

poached sea bass & salsa

Calories per serving **205**
Serves **4**
Preparation time **15 minutes**
Cooking time **25 minutes**

2 inch piece of **fresh ginger
root**, peeled and thinly sliced
2 **lemon grass stalks**, sliced
lengthwise
1 **lime**, sliced
¾ cup **dry sherry**
2 tablespoons **fish sauce**
2 **sea bass**, about 1¼ lb each,
cleaned and scaled

Salsa
3 firm **tomatoes**
1 **lemon grass stalk**, outer
leaves discarded, finely
sliced
½ inch piece of **fresh ginger
root**, peeled and finely
grated
2 tablespoons chopped
cilantro
2 **scallions**, chopped
2 teaspoons **peanut oil**
1 tablespoon **lime juice**
1½ teaspoons **light soy
sauce**

Put the ginger, lemon grass, lime, sherry, fish sauce, and enough water to just cover the fish in a fish kettle or large skillet. Bring to a boil, then reduce the heat and simmer gently for 5 minutes.

Place the sea bass in the fish kettle or on a large piece of nonstick parchment paper if using a skillet. Lower into the stock, adding more water if necessary so that it covers the fish. Bring the stock to a boil and then turn off the heat. Cover and let poach for 15 minutes or until the fish flakes easily when pressed in the center with a knife.

Meanwhile, make the salsa. Seed and finely dice the tomatoes and place in a bowl with the lemon grass, ginger, cilantro, and scallions. Stir through the oil, lime juice, and soy sauce and let infuse.

Lift the poached sea bass carefully from the cooking liquid onto a plate. Peel away the skin and gently lift the tenderloins from the bones. Place on a serving dish with the salsa and serve with steamed rice and lime wedges, if desired.

For pan-fried sea bass with salsa, ask the fish merchant to tenderloin the whole sea bass. Heat 1 tablespoon olive oil in a nonstick skillet and pan-fry the sea bass tenderloins over medium-high heat, skin side down, for 3–4 minutes. Reduce the heat, cover, and cook for another 3–4 minutes or until cooked through. Serve with the salsa. **Calories per serving 223**

thai red pork & bean curry

Calories per serving **216**
Serves **4**
Preparation time **10 minutes**
Cooking time **5 minutes**

2 tablespoons **peanut oil**
1½ tablespoons prepared
   Thai red curry paste
12 oz **lean pork**, sliced into
   thin strips
2 cups **green beans**, topped
   and cut in half
2 tablespoons **Thai fish sauce
   (nam pla)**
1 teaspoon **sugar**
Chinese chives or **regular
   chives**, to garnish

Heat the oil in a wok over medium heat until the oil starts to shimmer. Add the curry paste and cook, stirring, until it releases its aroma.

Add the pork and green beans and stir-fry for 2–3 minutes, until the meat is cooked through and the beans are just tender.

Stir in the fish sauce and sugar and serve, garnished with Chinese chives or regular chives.

For chicken green curry with sugar snap peas, cook as above, replacing the red curry paste with 1½ tablespoons green curry paste, the pork with 12 oz sliced chicken breast and the green beans with 2 cups sliced sugar snap peas. Add a dash of lime juice before serving. **Calories per serving 204**

bass with tomato & basil sauce

Calories per serving **237**
Serves **4**
Preparation time **10 minutes**
Cooking time **30 minutes**

8 **plum tomatoes**, halved
2 tablespoons **lemon juice**
grated zest of **1 lemon**, plus
   extra to garnish
4 **sea bass tenderloins**, about
   5 oz each
2 tablespoons chopped **basil**
2 tablespoons **extra virgin
   olive oil**
salt and **pepper**

To garnish
basil leaves
lemon wedges

Make the sauce up to 2 days in advance. Arrange the tomatoes in a roasting pan, season well with salt and pepper, and cook in a preheated oven, 400°F, for 20 minutes.

Transfer the tomatoes and any cooking juices to a saucepan and heat through gently with the lemon juice and zest. Season to taste and set aside until ready to serve.

Season the fish tenderloins and cook under a preheated hot broiler for approximately 10 minutes or until the fish is cooked through.

Meanwhile, warm the sauce through. Stir the basil and oil through the sauce and spoon it over the fish. Garnish with basil leaves, more grated lemon zest, and lemon wedges.

For jumbo shrimp in tomato & basil sauce, replace the bass tenderloins with 16 raw and peeled jumbo shrimp. Sauté the shrimp in a little oil spray until pink and cooked through. Make the sauce as above and spoon over the top of the cooked shrimp to serve.
Calories per serving 169

russian borsch

Calories per serving **259**
Serves **6**
Preparation time **15 minutes**
Cooking time **55 minutes**

2 tablespoons **butter**
1 tablespoon **sunflower oil**
1 **onion**, finely chopped
12 oz uncooked **beets**,
   trimmed, peeled, and diced
2 **carrots**, diced
2 **celery sticks**, diced
1½ cups chopped **red
   cabbage**
2 cups diced **potatoes**
2 **garlic cloves**, finely chopped
6 cups **beef stock**
1 tablespoon **tomato paste**
6 tablespoons **red wine
   vinegar**
1 tablespoon packed **brown
   sugar**
2 **bay leaves**
salt and **pepper**

To serve
¾ cup **sour cream**
small bunch of **dill weed**

Heat the butter and oil in a saucepan, add the onion, and cook for 5 minutes, until softened. Add the beets, carrot, celery, red cabbage, potatoes, and garlic and cook for 5 minutes, stirring frequently.

Stir in the stock, tomato paste, vinegar, and sugar. Add the bay leaves and season well with salt and pepper. Bring to a boil, then cover and simmer for 45 minutes, until the vegetables are tender. Discard the bay leaves, then taste and adjust the seasoning if needed.

Ladle into bowls and top with spoonfuls of sour cream, torn dill fronds, and a little black pepper. Serve with rye bread, if desired.

For vegetarian borsch with pinched dumplings,
soak 1½ oz dried mushrooms in 1¼ cups boiling water for 15 minutes. Make up the soup as above, omitting the beef stock, adding the soaked mushrooms and their liquid plus 5 cups vegetable stock instead. For the dumplings, mix 1 cup white flour, ¼ teaspoon caraway seeds, salt and pepper, 2 beaten eggs, and enough water to mix to a smooth dough. Shape into a sausage, pinch off pieces and add to the soup, simmering for 10 minutes until spongy. Omit the cream and dill and serve. **Calories per serving 277**

malaysian coconut vegetables

Calories per serving **251**
Serves **4**
Preparation time **15 minutes, plus soaking**
Cooking time **20 minutes**

½ cup **broccoli florets**
1 cup **green beans**, cut into 1 inch lengths
1 **red bell pepper**, cored, seeded, and sliced
1 **zucchini**, thinly sliced

Coconut sauce
2 tablespoons **tamarind pulp**
⅔ cup **boiling water**
1 (12 oz) can **coconut milk**
2 teaspoons **Thai green curry paste**
½ inch piece of **fresh ginger root**, peeled and finely grated
1 **onion**, cut into small cubes
½ teaspoon **ground turmeric**
salt

Make the coconut sauce. Put the tamarind in a bowl. Pour over the measured water and let soak for 30 minutes. Mash the tamarind in the water, then push through a fine-mesh strainer set over another bowl, squashing the tamarind so that you get as much of the pulp as possible; discard the stringy bits and any seeds.

Take 2 tablespoons of the cream from the top of the coconut milk and pour it into a wok or large skillet. Add the curry paste, ginger, onion, and turmeric, and cook over gentle heat, stirring, for 2–3 minutes. Stir in the rest of the coconut milk and the tamarind water. Bring to a boil, then reduce the heat to a simmer and add a pinch of salt.

Add the broccoli to the coconut sauce and cook for 5 minutes, then add the green beans and red pepper. Cook, stirring, for another 5 minutes. Finally, stir in the zucchini and cook gently for 1–2 minutes, until the zucchini is just tender. Serve immediately with some crispy shrimp crackers, if desired.

For chicken & green beans in coconut sauce,
soak the tamarind and make the coconut sauce as above. Add 1 lb diced boneless, skinless chicken breast to the wok or skillet. Simmer for 5 minutes, then add the sliced green beans, omitting the bell pepper and zucchini. Simmer gently for another 5 minutes until the chicken is cooked through. **Calories per serving 365**

cod & eggplant tapenade

Calories per serving **259**
Serves **4**
Preparation time **12 minutes**
Cooking time **35–40 minutes**

1 **eggplant**, cut into chunks
1 **garlic clove**, sliced
olive oil spray
4 thick, line-caught **cod tenderloins**, about 5 oz each
finely grated zest of ½ **lemon**
2 teaspoons finely chopped **lemon thyme**
2 teaspoons **olive oil**
1–2 tablespoons **black olive tapenade**
1–2 tablespoons fat-free **Greek yogurt**
2 tablespoons **pine nuts**, lightly toasted (optional)
salt and **pepper**

Put the eggplant in a foil-lined roasting pan, sprinkle with the garlic, season with salt and pepper, and spray with a little olive oil. Cover tightly with foil and place in a preheated oven, 350°F, for 35–40 minutes or until the eggplant is tender.

Meanwhile, place a cod tenderloin in the center of a piece of foil or nonstick parchment paper. Sprinkle with a little lemon zest, lemon thyme, and season with salt and pepper. Drizzle over ½ teaspoon of the olive oil, then fold the foil or paper over several times to make a small parcel. Repeat with the remaining cod tenderloins. Place the parcels on a baking sheet and bake in the oven 12 minutes before the end of the eggplant cooking time, until the fish is just cooked through. Let rest.

Remove the eggplant from the oven and place in a food processor or blender with the black olive tapenade and Greek yogurt. Blend until almost smooth, season to taste, and scrape into a bowl.

Serve the cod on a bed of steamed green beans, sprinkled with the pine nuts, if using, and with the eggplant and yogurt puree on the side.

For baked lemon sole & capers, place 4 lemon sole tenderloins on a large, foil-lined baking sheet. Sprinkle with the lemon zest, lemon thyme, and 1 teaspoon rinsed and drained capers, chopped. Drizzle with the olive oil, then season with pepper. Cover tightly with foil and place in the preheated oven for 8–10 minutes or until the fish is just cooked and flakes easily. Serve as above. **Calories per serving 262**

recipes
under 400
calories

moroccan broiled sardines

Calories per serving **302**
Serves **4**
Preparation time **10 minutes**
Cooking time **6–8 minutes**

12 **sardines**, cleaned and
   gutted
2 tablespoons **harissa**
2 tablespoons **olive oil**
juice of 1 **lemon**
salt flakes and **pepper**
chopped **cilantro**, to garnish
lemon wedges, to serve

Heat the broiler on the hottest setting. Rinse the sardines and pat dry with paper towels. Make 3 deep slashes on both sides of each fish with a sharp knife.

Mix the harissa with the oil and lemon juice to make a thin paste. Rub into the sardines on both sides. Put the sardines on a lightly oiled baking sheet. Cook under the broiler for 3–4 minutes on each side, depending on their size, or until cooked through. Season to taste with salt flakes and pepper and serve immediately garnished with cilantro and with lemon wedges for squeezing over.

For baked sardines with pesto, line a medium ovenproof dish with 2 sliced tomatoes and 2 sliced onions. Prepare the sardines as above, then rub 4 tablespoons pesto over the fish and arrange in a single layer on top of the tomatoes and onions. Cover with foil and bake in a preheated oven, 400°F, for 20–25 minutes or until the fish is cooked through. **Calories per serving 375**

beef tenderloin with pepper crust

Calories per serving **302 (not including wholegrain rice)**

Serves **4**

Preparation time **15 minutes**

Cooking time **about 30 minutes**

1 **red pepper**, halved and seeded

2 **garlic cloves**

8 dry **black ripe olives**, pitted

1 tablespoon **olive oil**

2 teaspoons **capers**

8 **shallots**, peeled

3 tablespoons **balsamic vinegar**

1 teaspoon **light brown sugar**

4 **beef tenderloin steaks**, about 5 oz each

salt and **pepper**

Cook the bell pepper under a preheated hot broiler until the skin blackens. Remove and cover with damp paper towels until it is cool enough to handle, then peel the skin off and chop.

Blend together the garlic, olives, 1 teaspoon oil, the capers, and the chopped red pepper.

Put the shallots and the remaining oil in a small saucepan. Cover and cook, stirring frequently, over low heat for 15 minutes. Add the vinegar and sugar and cook uncovered, stirring frequently, for another 5 minutes.

Season the steaks with salt and pepper and cook, 2 at a time, in a preheated heavy skillet or ridged grill pan. Cook on one side for 2 minutes, then transfer to a baking sheet. Top each steak with some red pepper mix. Bake in a preheated oven, 400°F, for 5 minutes, or according to taste. Let stand in a warm place for 5 minutes before serving with the balsamic shallots and, if desired, steamed whole-grain rice.

For beef tenderloin with mushroom crust, blend 12 oz chopped mushrooms with 2 crushed garlic cloves, 1 chopped onion, 1 tablespoon olive oil, and seasoning. Cook as above for 10 minutes or until reduced down to concentrate. Add juice of ½ lemon, 2 tablespoons chopped fresh parsley, and a dash of brandy, then cook for another 5 minutes. Cook the steaks as above and top with the mushroom mixture. **Calories per serving 271**

chicken with red wine & grapes

Calories per serving **368**
Serves **4**
Preparation time **5 minutes**
Cooking time **30 minutes**

3 tablespoons **olive oil**
4 **skinless chicken breast
    tenderloins**, about 5 oz each
1 **red onion**, sliced
2 tablespoons **red pesto** (see
    below for homemade)
1¼ cups **red wine**
1¼ cups **water**
½ cup **red grapes**, halved and
    seeded
salt and **black pepper**
basil leaves, to garnish

Heat 2 tablespoons of the oil in a large skillet, add
the chicken breasts and cook over medium heat for
5 minutes, turning frequently, until browned all over.
Remove from the pan with a slotted spoon and drain
on paper towels.

Heat the remaining oil in the pan, add the onion slices
and pesto and cook, stirring constantly, for 3 minutes,
until the onion is softened but not browned.

Add the wine and measured water to the pan and
bring to a boil. Return the chicken breasts to the pan
and season with salt and pepper to taste. Reduce the
heat and simmer for 15 minutes, or until the chicken is
cooked through.

Stir in the grapes and serve immediately, garnished with
basil leaves.

For homemade red pesto, put 1 chopped garlic clove,
½ teaspoon sea salt, 1 cup basil leaves, 1 cup drained
sundried tomatoes in oil, ½ cup extra virgin olive oil,
and a little pepper in a food processor or blender
and blend until smooth. Transfer to a bowl and stir in
2 tablespoons freshly grated Parmesan cheese.
Calories per serving 368

hoisin pork stir-fry

Calories per serving **395**
Serves **2**
Preparation time **8 minutes**
Cooking time **6–8 minutes**

1 tablespoon **hoisin sauce**
1 tablespoon **light soy sauce**
1 tablespoon **white wine
   vinegar**
1 tablespoon **vegetable oil**
2 **garlic cloves**, sliced
½ inch piece of **fresh ginger
   root**, peeled and finely
   grated
1 small **red chile**, seeded and
   sliced
8 oz **pork tenderloin**, thinly
   sliced
1½ cups **sugar snap peas**
¾ cup **broccoli florets**
2 tablespoons **water**

Combine the hoisin and soy sauces and vinegar in
a bowl and set aside.

Heat the oil in a wok or large skillet, until starting
to smoke, add the garlic, ginger, and chile and stir-fry
over high heat for 10 seconds. Add the pork tenderloin
and stir-fry for 2–3 minutes, until golden. Remove with
a slotted spoon.

Add the sugar snap peas and broccoli florets to the pan
and stir-fry for 1 minute. Add the measured water and
cook for another 1 minute.

Return the pork to the pan, add the sauce mixture,
and cook for 1 minute, until the vegetables are cooked.
Serve with steamed rice.

For roasted hoisin pork, make the hoisin mixture
as above. Brush the sauce over 4 pieces of pork
tenderloin, about 6 oz each, in a roasting pan and
roast in a preheated oven, 400°F, for 15 minutes. Let
rest for 5 minutes, then serve with steamed green
vegetables and boiled rice. **Calories per serving 428**

spanish fish stew

Calories per serving **328**

Serves **4**

Preparation time **12 minutes**

Cooking time **about 25 minutes**

2 tablespoons **olive oil**

1 large **red onion**, sliced

4 **garlic cloves**, chopped

1 teaspoon **smoked paprika** or **hot smoked paprika**

pinch of **saffron threads**

11½ oz **angler fish tenderloin**, cut into chunks

8 oz **red mullet** or **goatfish tenderloins**, cut into large chunks

3 tablespoons **dry** or **medium-dry Madeira**

1 cup **fish** or **vegetable stock**

2 tablespoons **tomato paste**

1 (14½ oz) can **diced tomatoes**

2 **bay leaves**

1½ lb **live mussels**, scrubbed and debearded (discard any that don't shut when tapped) or 8 oz **cooked shelled mussels**

salt and **pepper**

3 tablespoons chopped **parsley**, to garnish

Heat the oil in a large, heavy saucepan over medium-low heat, add the onion and garlic, and cook gently for 8–10 minutes or until softened.

Stir in the paprika and saffron and cook for another minute. Stir in the fish, then pour over the Madeira. Add the stock, tomato paste, tomatoes, and bay leaves and season with salt and pepper. Bring to a boil, then reduce the heat and simmer gently for 5 minutes.

Stir in the live mussels, cover and cook over low heat for about 3 minutes or until they have opened. Discard any that remain closed. Alternatively, if using cooked shelled mussels, simmer the stew for 2–3 minutes more, or until the fish is cooked and tender, then stir in the cooked mussels. Cook for 30 seconds or until the mussels are heated through and piping hot.

Ladle into bowls and sprinkle with the parsley. Serve immediately with crusty bread.

For pan-fried red mullet with tomato sauce,

cook the onion and garlic with the spices as above. Pour in the Madeira and add the tomatoes, finely grated zest of ½ lemon, a pinch of sugar and season with salt and pepper. Simmer for 15–20 minutes. Heat 1–2 tablespoons olive oil in a nonstick skillet, add 1 lb red mullet (or goatfish) tenderloins, skin side down, and fry for 2–3 minutes or until crisp. Cover, reduce the heat, and cook for another 2 minutes or until the fish is just cooked through. Serve with the tomato sauce. **Calories per serving 330**

crab & grapefruit salad

Calories per serving **384**

Serves **4**

Preparation time **10 minutes**

13 oz **white crab meat**

1 **pink grapefruit**, peeled and
   sliced

1¼ cups **arugula**

3 **scallions**, sliced

2 cups **snow peas**, halved

salt and **pepper**

Watercress dressing

2 cups **watercress**, tough
   stalks removed

1 tablespoon **Dijon mustard**

2 tablespoon **olive oil**

To serve

4 **chapattis**

lime wedges

Combine the crabmeat, grapefruit, arugula, scallions,
and snow peas in a serving dish. Season with salt and
pepper to taste.

Make the dressing by blending together the watercress,
mustard, and oil. Season with salt.

Toast the chapattis. Stir the dressing into the salad and
serve with the toasted chapattis and lime wedges on
the side.

For shrimp, potato & asparagus salad, substitute
13 oz cooked peeled shrimp for the crab and
3½ oz cooked asparagus for the grapefruit, and add
7 oz cooked and cooled potatoes. **Calories per
serving 343**

spiced beef & vegetable stew

Calories per serving **325**
Serves **4**
Preparation time **15 minutes**
Cooking time **2½ hours**

1 lb **lean braising** or **stewing steak**
2 tablespoons **canola** or **olive oil**
1 large **onion**, chopped
1 inch piece of **fresh ginger root**, peeled and finely grated
2 **chiles**, sliced
2 **garlic cloves**, crushed
1½ cups **beef stock**
5 **star anise**
1 teaspoon **Chinese five-spice powder**
1 **cinnamon stick**
1 teaspoon **fennel seeds**
2 **dried kaffir lime leaves**
1 **lemon grass stalk**, chopped
1 teaspoon **black peppercorns**
2 tablespoons **shoyu** or **tamari sauce**
13 oz **carrots**, cut into ½ inch slices
1 lb **mooli** or **turnips**, cut into ½ inch slices
Chinese chives or **regular chives**, to garnish

Cut the steak into 1 inch cubes.

Heat the oil in a wok over medium heat. Add the onion, ginger, and chiles and stir-fry for 5–7 minutes.

Turn the heat up to high, add the beef, and stir-fry for 5–10 minutes, until lightly browned, stirring occasionally.

Add the garlic, stock, star anise, Chinese five-spice powder, cinnamon, fennel seeds, lime leaves, lemon grass, peppercorns, and shoyu sauce and stir well. Bring the mixture back to a boil, then turn the heat down, cover the pan and simmer gently for 1½ hours, stirring occasionally. Add the carrots and mooli and continue cooking, covered, for another 45 minutes or until the vegetables have softened.

Skim any fat off the surface and garnish with the chives before serving.

For sesame broccoli, to accompany the stew, blanch 2 cups broccoli florets in a saucepan of boiling water for 2 minutes, then drain and place on a serving dish. Make a dressing by combining 1 teaspoon sesame oil, 1 tablespoon shoyu sauce, and 1 crushed garlic clove, and pour it over the broccoli. Just before serving, sprinkle the dish with 1 tablespoon toasted sesame seeds. **Calories per serving 69**

lamb tenderloin with vegetables

Calories per serving **317**
Serves **4**
Preparation time **20 minutes**
Cooking time **35–45 minutes**

1 lb even-size **baby new potatoes**
1 tablespoon chopped **rosemary**
13 oz **lamb tenderloin**, diced
3 **garlic cloves**, halved
1 (14 oz) can **artichokes**, drained, rinsed, and halved
1 **red bell pepper**, seeded and quartered
7 oz small **leeks**
salt and **pepper**

Put the potatoes in a saucepan with plenty of lightly salted water and bring to a boil. Drain immediately and toss with the rosemary.

Transfer the potatoes to a roasting pan with the lamb, garlic, artichokes, and bell peppers. Cover and cook in a preheated oven, 350°F, for 30–40 minutes or until cooked through and the potato skins are golden. Meanwhile, steam the leeks.

Drain the excess fat and serve the lamb with the roasted vegetables, leeks, and any pan juices.

For herbed baked lamb, before baking sprinkle the diced lamb with 6–8 tablespoons lemon juice, ¼ teaspoon each dried oregano and thyme, the leaves torn from 2 oregano sprigs, 4 lemon thyme sprigs, and salt and pepper. **Calories per serving 319**

tuna layered lasagna

Calories per serving **335**
Serves **4**
Preparation time **10 minutes**
Cooking time **10 minutes**

8 dried **lasagna** sheets
1 tablespoon **olive oil**
1 bunch of **scallions**, sliced
2 **zucchini**, diced
2 cups **cherry tomatoes**,
  quartered
2 (7 oz) cans **tuna** in water,
  drained
1½ cups **arugula**
4 teaspoons **pesto**
pepper
basil leaves, to garnish

Cook the pasta sheets, in batches, in a large saucepan of salted boiling water according to the package instructions until al dente. Drain and return to the pan to keep warm.

Meanwhile, heat the oil in a skillet over a medium heat, add the scallions and zucchini and cook, stirring, for 3 minutes. Remove the pan from the heat, add the tomatoes, tuna, and arugula and gently toss everything together.

Place a little of the tuna mixture on 4 serving plates and top each with a pasta sheet. Spoon over the remaining tuna mixture, then top with the remaining pasta sheets. Season with plenty of pepper and top each with a spoonful of pesto and some basil leaves before serving.

For salmon lasagna, use 14 oz salmon tenderloins. Pan-fry the tenderloins for 2–3 minutes on each side or until they are cooked through, remove any bones and the skin, then flake and use in place of the tuna. Calories per serving 443

deviled tenderloin steaks

Calories per serving **336**
Serves **4**
Preparation time **10 minutes**
Cooking time **10 minutes**

2 tablespoons **olive oil**
4 **tenderloin steaks**, about
    6 oz each
1/3 cup **balsamic vinegar**
1/4 cup **full-bodied red wine**
4 tablespoons **beef stock**
2 **garlic cloves**, chopped
1 teaspoon crushed **fennel**
    seeds
1 tablespoon **sundried**
    tomato paste
1/2 teaspoon **dried red pepper**
    flakes
salt and **pepper**

To garnish
chopped **flat-leaf parsley**
arugula leaves (optional)

Heat the oil in a nonstick skillet until smoking hot. Add the steaks and cook over very high heat for about 2–3 minutes on each side, if you want your steaks to be medium rare, 4–5 minutes for medium, and 6–7 minutes for well done. Remove to a plate, season with salt and pepper, and keep warm in a low oven.

Pour the vinegar, wine, and stock into the pan and boil for 30 seconds, scraping any sediment from the bottom of the pan. Add the garlic and fennel seeds and whisk in the sundried tomato paste and pepper flakes. Bring the sauce to a boil and boil fast to reduce until syrupy.

Transfer the steaks to warmed serving plates, pouring any collected meat juices into the sauce. Return the sauce to a boil, then season with salt and pepper.

Pour the sauce over the steaks and serve immediately, garnished with chopped parsley and arugula leaves, if desired. Slice the steaks before serving, if you wish.

For deviled chicken breasts, heat the oil and use to cook 4 skinned chicken breasts for 5 minutes on each side. Leaving the chicken in the pan, follow the recipe above, replacing the beef stock with 1/4 cup chicken stock and using 1/2 teaspoon dried oregano instead of the fennel seeds. **Calories per serving 276**

shrimp & scallops with asparagus

Calories per serving **336**
Serves **4**
Preparation time **5 minutes**
Cooking time **10 minutes**

12 raw peeled **jumbo shrimp**
8 **scallops**
3 tablespoons **peanut oil**
1 inch piece **fresh ginger
root**, finely chopped
2 **garlic cloves**, crushed
8 oz **asparagus**, cut into
    1 inch lengths
2 tablespoons **Chinese rice
wine** or **dry sherry**
1 tablespoon **malt vinegar**
1½ tablespoons **light soy
sauce**
2 teaspoons **sugar**
½ cup **water**
½ teaspoon **sesame oil**
salt and **white pepper**

Season the shrimp and scallops with salt and freshly ground white pepper.

Heat 1 tablespoon of the oil in a wok over high heat until the oil starts to shimmer. Add the shrimp and stir-fry for 2 minutes, until they begin to color, then remove using a slotted spoon and set aside. Add another tablespoon of the oil to the wok and, once it is hot, stir-fry the scallops for 1 minute on each side. Remove using a slotted spoon and set aside.

Heat the remaining oil in the wok. Stir in the ginger, garlic, and asparagus and stir-fry for 1 minute, then add the rice wine, vinegar, soy sauce, sugar, and water and bring to a boil. Return the shrimp and scallops to the wok and stir-fry until they are cooked and the asparagus is just tender. Add the sesame oil and give everything a good stir, then serve.

For jumbo shrimp with peppers & sesame
seeds, use 16 raw peeled jumbo shrimp instead of the scallops. Replace the asparagus with 1 red and 1 yellow bell pepper, cored, seeded, and cut into thin strips. Cook as above, finishing with 2 tablespoons toasted sesame seeds. **Calories per serving 389**

gingery pork chops

Calories per serving **389**
Serves **4**
Preparation time **15 minutes**
Cooking time **20 minutes**

4 lean **pork chops**, about
    5 oz each
1½ inch piece of **fresh ginger**
    root, peeled and grated
1 teaspoon **sesame oil**
1 tablespoon **dark soy sauce**
2 teaspoons **stem ginger**
    syrup or **honey**

Dressing
1½ tablespoons **light soy**
    sauce
juice of 1 **blood orange**
2 pieces of **stem ginger**, finely
    chopped

Salad
2 large **carrots**, peeled and
    coarsely shredded
1¼ cups **snow peas**,
    shredded
1 cup **bean sprouts**
2 **scallions**, thinly sliced
2 tablespoons **unsalted**
    peanuts, coarsely chopped
    (optional)

Place the pork in a shallow ovenproof dish and rub with the ginger, sesame oil, soy sauce, and stem ginger syrup or honey until well covered. Let them marinate for 10 minutes.

Make the dressing. Mix together all the ingredients in a bowl and set aside for the flavors to develop.

Cook the pork in a preheated oven, 350°F, for 18–20 minutes or until cooked through but still juicy.

Meanwhile, mix the carrots, snow peas, bean sprouts, and scallions in a large bowl. Just before serving, toss with the dressing and pile into serving dishes. Sprinkle with the peanuts, if using, and top with the pork chops, drizzled with cooking juices. Serve immediately with steamed rice.

For pork & ginger stir-fry, replace the pork chops with 4 lean boneless pork loin chops and thinly slice. Cut the carrots into matchsticks. Heat 1–2 teaspoons sesame oil in a hot wok or large skillet, add the pork and stir-fry until just cooked. Add the carrots, snow peas, bean sprouts, and scallions and stir-fry for another 1–2 minutes. Toss with the dressing and serve immediately, sprinkled with the peanuts, if desired.
Calories per serving 369

turkey & avocado salad

Calories per serving **345 (not including rye or flat bread)**
Serves **4**
Preparation time **15 minutes**

12 oz cooked **turkey**
1 large **avocado**
pack of **garden cress**
4 cups **mixed salad greens**
5 tablespoons **mixed toasted seeds**, such as **pumpkin** and **sunflower**

Dressing
2 tablespoons **apple juice**
2 tablespoons **plain yogurt**
1 teaspoon **honey**
1 teaspoon **whole-grain mustard**
salt and **pepper**

Thinly slice the turkey. Peel, pit, and dice the avocado and mix it with the cress and salad greens in a large bowl. Add the turkey and toasted seeds and stir to combine.

Make the dressing by whisking together the apple juice, yogurt, honey, and mustard. Season to taste with salt and pepper.

Pour the dressing over the salad and toss to coat. Serve the salad with toasted wholegrain rye bread or rolled up in flat breads.

For crab, apple & avocado salad, prepare the salad in the same way, using 10 oz cooked, fresh white crabmeat instead of the turkey. Cut 1 apple into thin matchsticks and toss with a little lemon juice to stop it from discoloring. Make a dressing by whisking 2 tablespoons apple juice with 3 tablespoons olive oil, a squeeze of lemon juice, and 1 finely diced shallot. Season to taste with salt and pepper. Pour the dressing over the salad, stir carefully to mix, and serve. **Calories per serving 366**

flounder with sambal

Calories per serving **349**
Serves **4**
Preparation time **30 minutes,
plus marinating**
Cooking time **30 minutes**

1 small **lemon grass stalk**
2 **garlic cloves**, crushed
6 tablespoons **grated fresh
coconut**
2 **green chiles**, seeded and
finely chopped
4 **small whole flounder**,
scaled and gutted
4 tablespoons **oil**

Sambal
1 **onion**, finely chopped
1 **garlic clove**, crushed
1 tablespoon **oil**
2 tablespoons **grated fresh
coconut**
1 **red chile**, seeded and finely
chopped
2/3 cup **boiling water**
2 tablespoons **dried tamarind
pulp**
2 teaspoons **sugar**
1 tablespoon **white wine
vinegar**
1 tablespoon chopped **fresh
cilantro**

Finely chop the lemon grass stalk and mix with the garlic, coconut, and green chiles. Smear this dry mixture over each fish, then cover and let marinate in the refrigerator for 2 hours or overnight.

Make the coconut and tamarind sambal by gently sautéing the onion and garlic in the oil in a large skillet until softened. Add the coconut with the red chile, stir to coat in the oil, and cook for 2–3 minutes. Pour the measured water over the tamarind pulp in a heatproof bowl and stand for 10 minutes to dissolve.

Strain the juice from the tamarind pulp, mashing as much of the pulp through the strainer as possible. Add this juice to the pan with the sugar and simmer gently for 5 minutes. Add the vinegar, remove from the heat, and let cool. When cold, stir in the chopped cilantro. Turn into a bowl and wipe the pan clean.

Heat the oil in the pan and gently fry the flounder 2 at a time in the hot oil, turning once. After 6–8 minutes, when they are golden brown and cooked, remove from the oil and drain on paper towels. Keep warm while cooking the remaining fish. Serve the fish piping hot with the coconut and tamarind sambal.

For sugar snap salad, to serve as an accompaniment, blanch 10 oz sugar snap peas in boiling water for 1 minute, drain, refresh with cold water, and thinly slice. Place in a bowl with 3 chopped scallions, 1 tablespoon chopped cilantro leaves, and 1 tablespoon chopped mint. Drizzle with a dressing made from 1/2 a small finely sliced red chile, 2 tablespoons lime juice, 1 tablespoon fish sauce, and 1 tablespoon sugar. **Calories per serving 45**

beef strips with radicchio

Calories per serving **353**
Serves **4**
Preparation time **5 minutes**
Cooking time **5 minutes**

3 **sirloin steaks**, about 10 oz
   each
½ tablespoon **olive oil**
2 **garlic cloves**, finely chopped
5 oz **radicchio**, sliced into 1
   inch strips
salt

Trim the fat from the steaks and slice the meat into very thin strips.

Heat the oil in a heavy skillet over high heat, add the garlic and steak strips, season with salt, and stir-fry for 2 minutes or until the steak strips are golden brown.

Add the radicchio and stir-fry until the leaves are just beginning to wilt. Serve immediately.

For beef & caramelized onion couscous salad,

brush 1¼ lb beef tenderloin with 1 tablespoon olive oil, then sprinkle well with pepper. Heat a nonstick skillet over medium-high heat and cook the beef for 4 minutes on each side or until seared all over but still rare inside. Remove from the pan and let rest. To make the onion couscous, heat 2 tablespoons olive oil in the pan over medium heat, add 4 sliced onions and sauté, stirring occasionally, for 8–10 minutes or until softened. Meanwhile, put 1 cup couscous in a heatproof bowl and pour over 1½ cups boiling chicken or beef stock. Cover and let stand for 5 minutes or according to the package instructions, until the stock has been absorbed, then fluff up with a fork. Mix together 2 tablespoons Dijon mustard, 1 tablespoon olive oil, the juice of 1 lemon, and salt and pepper and toss with the couscous and onions. Slice the beef and place on top of the couscous. Serve with some arugula leaves on the side. **Calories per serving 498**

shrimp with garlicky beans

Calories per serving **389**
Serves **4**
Preparation time **10 minutes**
Cooking time **15 minutes**

3 tablespoons **olive oil**
1 **large onion**, finely chopped
3 **garlic cloves**, crushed
2 x 15 oz cans **cannellini,
  kidney** or **lima beans**,
  drained
½ cup **vegetable** or **fish stock**
13 oz raw peeled **shrimp**
½ teaspoon **mild sweet
  paprika**
2 tablespoons **tomato paste**
1 tablespoon chopped
  oregano
2 teaspoons **honey**
pepper

Heat 2 tablespoons of the oil in a saucepan, add the onion and sauté gently for 5 minutes. Add the garlic and sauté for another minute.

Remove the pan from the heat. Add the beans and use a potato masher to crush them. Add the stock and plenty of pepper and set aside.

Dust the shrimp with the paprika and a little salt. Heat the remaining oil in a skillet, add the shrimp, and cook for 5–6 minutes, turning once or twice during cooking, until they turn pink and are cooked through. Stir in the tomato paste, oregano, honey, and 2 tablespoons water and cook for 2–3 minutes or until it begins to bubble.

Meanwhile, reheat the pan with the beans until piping hot. Spoon the bean mixture into small dishes, pile the shrimp on top and pour over the cooking juices.

For blackened cod with garlicky beans, prepare and cook the beans as above. Spread one side of each of 4 x 6 oz cod tenderloins with 1 heaping teaspoon of prepared black olive tapenade. Heat 2 tablespoons olive oil in a ridged grill pan over medium heat, add the fish and cook for about 5 minutes on each side or until cooked through. Serve on a bed of crushed beans, and sprinkle with chopped black olives and parsley.
Calories per serving 331

chicken & tofu miso noodles

Calories per serving **359**
Serves **4**
Preparation time **10 minutes**
Cooking time **25 minutes**

2 (½ oz) packets **instant miso soup powder** or **paste**

3 cups **water**

2 **star anise**

2 tablespoons **fish sauce**

1 tablespoon **light soy sauce**

1 tablespoon **palm sugar** or packed **light brown sugar**

1 **red chile**, seeded and sliced (optional)

7 oz **baby corn**

1 cup **snow peas**

8 oz **cooked chicken breast**, torn

7 oz **firm silken tofu**, cut into ½ inch cubes

5½ oz **enoki mushrooms**, or **shiitake mushrooms**, thinly sliced

13 oz **fresh egg noodles**

1 **scallion**, very finely sliced, to garnish (optional)

Place the miso powder or paste in a large saucepan with the measured water, star anise, fish sauce, soy sauce, sugar, and chile, if using. Bring to a boil, then reduce the heat and simmer gently for 15 minutes.

Stir in the baby corn and snow peas and cook for another 3 minutes or until almost tender. Remove the pan from the heat, stir in the chicken, tofu, and mushrooms and cover to retain the heat.

Cook the noodles in a large saucepan of boiling water for 3–4 minutes, or according to the package instructions, until tender. Drain well and divide between deep bowls, then ladle over the hot soup and serve immediately, garnished with the scallion, if desired.

For chicken, tofu & mushroom stir-fry, heat 2 tablespoons peanut oil in a smoking hot wok or large skillet. Stir-fry the baby corn and snow peas for 2 minutes or until beginning to wilt. Add the chicken, tofu, and mushrooms and stir-fry for 1–2 minutes or until hot and the mushrooms are tender. Stir in 1 (11½ oz) jar of black bean stir-fry sauce, toss briefly and serve with the cooked noodles, sprinkled with scallions. **Calories per serving 470**

korean beef with cucumber

Calories per serving **362**
Serves **4**
Preparation time **12 minutes,
   plus marinating**
Cooking time **10 minutes**

1 lb **sirloin steak**, trimmed and
   cut into thin strips
2 teaspoons **sesame oil**
2 tablespoons **light soy sauce**
½ teaspoon **salt**
1 teaspoon **sugar**
2 **garlic cloves**, crushed
1 tablespoon chopped **fresh
   ginger root**
1 **cucumber**
3 tablespoons **peanut oil**
4 **scallions**, finely sliced on
   the diagonal
2 tablespoons toasted
   sesame seeds, to garnish

Marinate the beef for 30 minutes in a bowl with the
sesame oil, soy sauce, salt, sugar, garlic, and ginger.

Peel the cucumber, cut it in half lengthwise and then
into ½ inch slices.

Heat half the oil in a wok over high heat until the
oil starts to shimmer. Add half the beef and stir-fry
for 2–3 minutes, until just cooked, then remove using
a slotted spoon.

Heat the remaining oil and stir-fry the rest of the beef
in the same way.

Add the cucumber and scallions. Stir-fry for another
1 minute, until the cucumber is only slightly tender,
and serve garnished with a sprinkling of toasted
sesame seeds.

For spiced pork with cucumber, replace the beef with
1 lb lean pork, cut into strips. Add 1 tablespoon crushed
cilantro seeds to the marinade ingredients and prepare
the dish as above. Finish by tossing 1 red chile, cut into
thin rounds, a handful of cilantro leaves, and the juice of
½ lime into the finished dish. **Calories per serving 346**

chinese-style turkey wraps

Calories per serving **365**
Serves **2**
Preparation time **10 minutes**
Cooking time **1–2 minutes**

½ teaspoon **vegetable oil**
3½ oz **turkey breast**, thinly
    sliced
1 tablespoon **honey**
2 tablespoons **soy sauce**
1 tablespoon **sesame oil**
2 soft **flour tortillas**
½ cup **bean sprouts**
¼ **red bell pepper**, cored,
    seeded, and thinly sliced
¼ **onion**, thinly sliced
¼ cup **snow peas**, sliced
2 **baby corn ears**, thinly sliced

Heat the oil in a skillet over moderate heat and add the turkey to the pan. Stir for 1–2 minutes until cooked through. Reduce the heat and stir in the honey, soy sauce, and sesame oil, making sure that the turkey is well coated. Set aside to cool.

Assemble a wrap by placing half the turkey mixture down the center of a tortilla. Add half the bean sprouts and bell pepper, onion, snow peas, and baby corn. Repeat with the other tortilla. (Alternatively, retain the remaining tortilla and mixture for use another day; the mixture will keep for up to 24 hours in the refrigerator.)

Roll up the tortilla securely and wrap in nonstick parchment paper (plastic wrap can make the wrap rather soggy).

For Chinese-style pork & bok choy wraps, replace the turkey with 4 oz tenderloin pork strips tossed with ½ teaspoon Chinese five spice and cook as above for 3–4 minutes. Add 1 small head bok choy, shredded, with the honey, soy sauce, and sesame oil and cook for another 2 minutes. Assemble as above with 1 cup bean sprouts, omitting the snow peas, onion, and corn.
Calories per serving 389

broiled lamb with caperberries

Calories per serving **308**
Serves **4**
Preparation time **10 minutes**
Cooking time **10 minutes**

4 **lamb leg steaks**, about
   4 oz each, fat trimmed off
6 tablespoons chopped
   flat-leaf parsley, plus extra
   whole sprigs to garnish
1 **garlic clove**, crushed
12 **sundried tomatoes**
1 tablespoon **lemon juice**
1 tablespoon **olive oil**
2 tablespoons **caperberries**,
   rinsed
salt and **pepper**

Season the meat with salt and pepper and cook under a preheated hot broiler for about 5 minutes on each side until golden.

Reserve 4 tablespoons of the chopped parsley. Blend the remaining parsley with the garlic, tomatoes, lemon juice, and oil.

Spoon the tomato sauce over the lamb. Sprinkle with the reserved chopped flat-leaf parsley and add the caperberries. Garnish with whole parsley sprigs and serve with pasta, if desired.

For grilled lamb with tapenade, use black olive tapenade instead of the dressing and stir all the parsley through it. To make your own tapenade, blend 1 cup pitted ripe black olives, 3 tablespoons extra virgin olive oil, 1 garlic clove, and 2 salted anchovies in a food processor with black pepper and add chopped flat-leaf parsley to taste. **Calories per serving 357**

chicken & adzuki bean salad

Calories per serving **376**
Serves **4**
Preparation time **15 minutes**
Cooking time **2–3 minutes**

1 **green bell pepper**, cored,
  seeded, and chopped
1 **red bell pepper**, cored,
  seeded, and chopped
1 small **red onion**, finely
  chopped
1 (14 oz) can **adzuki beans**,
  drained
1 (8 oz) can **corn kernels**,
  drained
1 small bunch of **cilantro**,
  chopped
1 cup unsweetened **coconut
  chips** or **flakes**
8 oz cooked **chicken breast**,
  shredded
small handful of **alfalfa shoots**
  (optional)

Dressing
3 tablespoons **light peanut oil**
2 tablespoons **light soy sauce**
1 inch piece of **fresh ginger
  root**, peeled and finely
  grated
1 tablespoon **rice vinegar**

Mix together the green and red peppers, onion, adzuki beans, corn kernels, and half the cilantro in a large bowl. Whisk together the dressing ingredients in a separate bowl, then stir 3 tablespoons into the bean salad. Spoon the salad into serving dishes.

Place the coconut chips or flakes in a nonstick skillet over medium heat and dry-fry for 2–3 minutes or until lightly golden brown, stirring continuously.

Sprinkle the shredded chicken and remaining cilantro leaves over the bean salad and top with the toasted coconut and alfalfa shoots, if using. Serve with the remaining dressing.

For shrimp, avocado & coconut salad, make as above, replacing the chicken with 8 oz cooked, peeled shrimp. Dice the flesh of 1 firm, ripe avocado, toss in 1 tablespoon of lime juice and add to the bean salad. Serve as above. **Calories per serving 458**

quick tuna steak with green salsa

Calories per serving **383 (not including crusty bread)**

Serves **4**

Preparation time **14 minutes, plus marinating**

Cooking time **2–4 minutes**

2 tablespoons **olive oil**

grated zest of 1 **lemon**

2 teaspoons chopped **parsley**

½ teaspoon crushed **cilantro seeds**

4 fresh **tuna steaks**, about 5 oz each

salt and **pepper**

Salsa

2 tablespoons **capers**, chopped

2 tablespoons chopped **cornichons**

1 tablespoon finely chopped **parsley**

2 teaspoons chopped **chives**

2 teaspoons finely chopped **chervil**

¼ cup pitted **green olives**, chopped

1 **shallot**, finely chopped (optional)

2 tablespoons **lemon juice**

2 tablespoons **olive oil**

Mix together the oil, lemon zest, parsley, and cilantro seeds with plenty of pepper in a bowl. Rub the tuna steaks with the mixture.

Combine the ingredients for the salsa, season with salt and pepper to taste and set aside.

Heat a ridged grill pan or skillet until hot and cook the tuna steaks for 1–2 minutes on each side to cook partially. The tuna should be well seared but rare. Remove and let rest for a couple of minutes.

Serve the tuna steaks with a spoonful of salsa, a dressed lettuce salad, and plenty of fresh crusty bread.

For yellow pepper & mustard salsa, combine the following: 2 yellow bell peppers, finely chopped; 1 tablespoon Dijon mustard; 2 tablespoons each finely chopped chives, parsley, and dill weed; 1 teaspoon sugar; 1 tablespoon cider vinegar; 2 tablespoons olive oil. **Calories per serving 46**

spicy pork, fried rice & greens

Calories per serving **384**
Serves **4**
Preparation time **15 minutes,
    plus marinating**
Cooking time **20 minutes**

1 cup **easy-cook basmati rice**
3 tablespoons **hoisin sauce**
2 **garlic cloves**, crushed
2 inch piece of **fresh ginger
    root**, grated
1 **red chile**, sliced
1 **star anise**
1 tablespoon **tomato paste**
10 oz **pork tenderloin**, cut
    into thin strips
sunflower oil spray
1 **red onion**, chopped
4 oz **cabbage** or **collard
    greens**, finely chopped
1 **carrot**, finely sliced
toasted sesame seeds,
    to serve

Mix together the hoisin sauce, garlic, ginger, chile, star anise, and tomato paste. Toss the pork in the mixture, cover and set aside for up to 1 hour.

Meanwhile, cook the rice in boiling salted water for 16–18 minutes or according to the package instructions. Drain and set aside.

Heat a wok over high heat and spray with oil. Remove the pork from the marinade (discard the remainder) and cook the meat in the wok for about 1 minute. Stir in the onion, cabbage, and carrot, then the rice. Toss and stir everything together over high heat for about 3 minutes, until the rice is hot. Sprinkle with sesame seeds and serve.

For hoisin lamb with stir-fry noodles, use 10 oz lamb tenderloin instead of pork and omit the rice and tomato paste. Marinate and stir-fry the lamb with the vegetables as above. Then add 3 x 5 oz packs straight-to-wok rice noodles (or dried rice noodles, cooked according to the package instructions) and stir-fry for about 1 minute, until hot. Sprinkle with chopped fresh cilantro leaves instead of sesame seeds and serve. **Calories per serving 345**

jumbo shrimp with japanese salad

Calories per serving **388**
Serves **4**
Preparation time **10 minutes,
  plus cooling**
Cooking time **3 minutes**

13 oz raw, peeled **jumbo
  shrimp**
2 cups **bean sprouts**
1 cups **snow peas**, shredded
½ cup thinly sliced **water
  chestnuts**
½ **iceberg lettuce**, shredded
12 **radishes**, thinly sliced
1 tablespoon **sesame seeds**,
  lightly toasted

Dressing
2 tablespoons **rice vinegar**
½ cup **sunflower oil**
1 teaspoon **five spice powder**
  (optional)
2 tablespoons **mirin**

Set a steamer over a pan of simmering water and steam the jumbo shrimp for 2–3 minutes, until cooked and pink. Set aside and let cool.

Make the dressing by mixing together all the ingredients in a small bowl.

Toss together the bean sprouts, snow peas, water chestnuts, lettuce, and radishes and place the shrimp and sesame seeds on top. Drizzle over the dressing and serve immediately.

For chili sauce to serve as an accompaniment, combine 1 finely chopped garlic clove, ½ teaspoon finely grated fresh ginger root, 2 teaspoons light soy sauce, 1 tablespoon sweet chili sauce, and ½ tablespoon ketchup. Mix well. **Calories per serving 19**

haddock parcels & coconut rice

Calories per serving **340**
Serves **4**
Preparation time **15 minutes**
Cooking time **20 minutes**

4 **haddock tenderloins**, about
    5 oz each
¼ cup chopped **fresh cilantro**
1 **red chile**, chopped
1 **shallot**, finely sliced
1 **lime**, sliced, plus extra lime
    halves to serve
2 **lemon grass stalks**,
    1 coarsely chopped and
    1 bashed
1 cup **Thai jasmine rice**
2 fresh or dried **kaffir lime
    leaves**
3 tablespoons **reduced-fat
    coconut milk**

Cut 4 pieces of nonstick parchment paper, each
12 inches square. Put a haddock tenderloin in the
center of each piece and arrange some of the cilantro,
chile, shallot, lime, and chopped lemon grass stalk
evenly over each. Wrap them up into neat parcels.

Transfer the parcels to a baking sheet and cook in
a preheated oven, 350°F, for 20 minutes.

Meanwhile, put the rice in a pan with 1⅔ cups water,
the bashed lemon grass stalk, and the lime leaves.
Cover and simmer for 12 minutes. When the rice is
cooked and the water absorbed, stir in the coconut
milk. Serve with the haddock parcels, with some extra
lime halves.

For salmon parcels with sesame rice, use
5 oz portions of skinless salmon tenderloin instead
of the haddock. Use lemon slices instead of lime and
omit the lemon grass. Sprinkle a few drops of sesame
oil over each salmon portion and cook as above. Omit
the lime leaves and coconut milk from the rice. Fork
2 tablespoons toasted sesame seeds and 2 chopped
scallions into the cooked rice and serve with the salmon,
adding lemon wedges for more zest. **Calories per
serving 493**

tomato & chorizo stew with clams

Calories per serving **355**
Serves **4**
Preparation time **15 minutes**
Cooking time **about**
  25 minutes

8 oz **chorizo** sausage, cut into
  chunks
1 teaspoon **cilantro seeds**,
  crushed
1 tablespoon **fennel seeds**,
  crushed
1 **onion**, finely chopped
1 **red chile**, seeded and finely
  chopped
2 **garlic cloves**, finely chopped
3 tablespoons **white wine**
1 (14½ oz) can **diced**
  tomatoes
¾ cup **fish stock**
1 lb **live clams**, cleaned
  (discard any that don't shut
  when tapped)
small handful of **basil leaves**,
  to garnish

Heat a large saucepan over high heat, add the chorizo
and fry until the natural oil has been released and the
chorizo is beginning to color. Remove with a slotted
spoon, leaving behind the oil, and set aside.

Add the cilantro and fennel seeds to the chorizo oil and
cook for 1 minute, then add the onion and chile and cook
until the onion has softened but not colored. Add the garlic
and fry for another minute.

Pour in the white wine and let bubble until just
1 tablespoon of liquid is left. Add the tomatoes and
stock and bring to a boil, then return the chorizo to the
pan. Add the clams, then cover and cook until the clams
have opened. Discard any that remain closed.

Ladle into bowls, sprinkle with a few basil leaves, and
serve with crusty bread, if desired.

For spicy bean stew with pan-fried Porgy, make the
stew as above, omitting the clams and chorizo and adding
1 (15 oz) can cannellini beans and 1 (15 oz) can kidney
beans, drained. Pan-fry 2 Porgy tenderloins and serve
with the bean stew. **Calories per serving 259**

pork with bell pepper & noodles

Calories per serving **314**
Serves **4**
Preparation time **30 minutes**
Cooking time **10 minutes**

5 oz **flat rice noodles**
sunflower oil spray
3 **scallions**, sliced
1 **red bell pepper**, diced
2 **kaffir lime leaves**, shredded
2 **red chiles**, seeded and
  sliced
½ **lemon grass stalk**, finely
  chopped
14½ oz **pork tenderloin**,
  shredded
2 tablespoons **soy sauce**
¾ cup **Thai fish sauce** (nam
  pla)
⅓ cup **palm sugar** or firmly
  packed **brown sugar**

To garnish
red or **green basil leaves**
shredded **scallions**

Cook the noodles according to the instructions on
the package.

Heat a wok or large skillet and lightly spray with oil.
Add the scallions, red pepper, lime leaves, chiles, and
lemon grass and stir-fry for 1 minute.

Add the shredded pork and stir-fry over high heat for
2 minutes. Add the soy sauce, fish sauce, sugar, and
drained noodles and cook for about 2 minutes, using
2 spoons to lift and stir until the noodles are evenly
coated and hot.

Serve immediately, garnished with basil leaves and
shredded scallions.

For pork with bell pepper, orange & honey, omit
the lime leaves, lemon grass stalk, fish sauce, and sugar.
Stir-fry the pork as above with the scallions, red pepper,
and chiles, then add the soy sauce, grated zest of
1 orange, and 3 teaspoons each fresh orange juice
and honey. Add the drained noodles and cook as
above. Serve garnished with orange wedges.
Calories per serving 319

swordfish with couscous & salsa

Calories per serving **399**
Serves **4**
Preparation time **10 minutes**
Cooking time **10 minutes**

4 **swordfish steaks**, about
   5 oz each
4–5 small ripe **tomatoes**
16 **Kalamata olives** in brine,
   drained
2 tablespoons chopped **flat-
   leaf parsley**
salt and **pepper**
1 cup **couscous**

Season the swordfish steaks with salt and pepper.

Dice or quarter the tomatoes and transfer them to a
bowl with all the juices. Remove the pits from the olives
and chop the flesh if the pieces are still large. Stir them
into the tomatoes with the parsley, season to taste, and
set aside.

Cook the couscous according to the instructions on
the package and set aside.

Meanwhile, cook the swordfish steaks, 2 at a time,
in a preheated hot ridged grill pan. Cook on the first side
for 4 minutes, without disturbing them, then turn and
cook for another minute.

Serve the swordfish and couscous immediately, topped
with the olive and tomato salsa.

For hake with pasta & salsa, replace the couscous
with 7 oz tagliatelle or baby pasta shapes and cook
according to the package instructions. Replace the
swordfish with 4 hake tenderloins and cook as
described above. When the pasta is cooked, toss with
extra chopped parsley and a handful of chopped capers.
Serve the hake and pasta as above, topped with the
salsa. **Calories per serving 366**

recipes under 500 calories

falafel pita pockets

Calories per serving **470**

Serves **4**

Preparation time **15 minutes, plus overnight soaking**

Cooking time **12 minutes**

1½ cups **dried chickpeas**
1 **small onion**, finely chopped
2 **garlic cloves**, crushed
½ bunch of **parsley**
½ bunch of **cilantro**
2 teaspoons **ground coriander**
½ teaspoon **baking powder**
2 tablespoons **vegetable oil**, for pan-frying
4 **whole-wheat pita breads**
handful of **salad greens**
2 **tomatoes**, diced
¼ cup **fat-free Greek yogurt**
salt and **pepper**

Put the chickpeas in a bowl, add cold water to cover by a generous 14 inches and let soak overnight.

Drain the chickpeas, transfer to a food processor and process until coarsely ground. Add the onion, garlic, fresh herbs, ground coriander, and baking powder. Season with salt and pepper and process until really smooth. Using wet hands, shape the mixture into 16 small patties.

Heat the vegetable oil in a large skillet over medium-high heat, add the patties, in batches, and cook for 3 minutes on each side or until golden and cooked through. Remove with a slotted spoon and drain on paper towels.

Split the pita breads and fill with the falafel, salad greens, and diced tomatoes. Add a spoonful of the yogurt to each and serve immediately.

For falafel salad, toss 4 handfuls of mixed salad leaves with a little olive oil, lemon juice, and salt and pepper and arrange on serving plates. Core, seed, and dice 1 red bell pepper and sprinkle it over the salads. Top with the falafel and spoon over a little yogurt. **Calories per serving 305**

shrimp, mango & avocado wrap

Calories per serving **409**

Serves **4**

Preparation time **10 minutes, plus standing**

2 tablespoons **low-fat crème fraîche** or **sour cream**

2 teaspoons **tomato ketchup**

few drops of **Tabasco sauce**, to taste

10 oz cooked peeled **shrimp**

1 **mango**, peeled, pitted, and thinly sliced

1 **avocado**, peeled, pitted, and sliced

4 flour **tortillas**

2 cups **watercress**

Mix together the crème fraîche, ketchup, and Tabasco to taste in a bowl.

Add the shrimp, mango, and avocado and toss the mixture together.

Spoon the mixture into the tortillas, add some sprigs of watercress, roll up and serve.

For tangy chicken wraps, marinate 10 oz chicken in a mixture of 1 tablespoon fresh lemon or lime juice, I tablespoon Worcestershire sauce, and 1 chopped garlic clove for 20 minutes. Cook the chicken under a preheated medium broiler for 10 minutes, turning often. Slice and use instead of the shrimp. **Calories per serving 461**

lamb stuffed with rice

Calories per serving **412**
Serves **4**
Preparation time **40 minutes**
Cooking time **1 hour**
   20 minutes

2 **red bell peppers**, cored,
   seeded, and halved
¼ cup **wild rice**, cooked
5 **garlic cloves**, chopped
5 **semi-dried tomatoes**,
   chopped
2 tablespoons chopped **flat-
   leaf parsley**
1¼ lb **boneless leg of lamb**,
   butterflied
4 **artichoke** halves
salt and **pepper**

Put the bell pepper halves in a roasting pan and cook
in a preheated oven, 350°F, for 20 minutes, until the
skin has blackened and blistered. Cover with damp
paper towels and set aside. When the peppers are cool
enough to handle, peel off the skin and chop the flesh.
(Leave the oven on.)

Mix together one of the chopped peppers, the rice,
garlic, tomatoes, and parsley. Season with salt and
pepper to taste.

Put the lamb on a board and make a horizontal incision,
almost all the way along, to make a cavity for stuffing.
Fold back the top half, spoon in the rice stuffing and
fold back the top. Secure with skewers.

Cook the lamb for 1 hour, basting frequently and
adding the artichokes and other chopped pepper for
the last 15 minutes of cooking time. Slice the lamb and
serve immediately with roasted new potatoes, if desired.

For lamb stuffed with cilantro & mint, combine
the grated zest and juice of 1 lime, 2 finely chopped
scallions, 2 tablespoons each chopped fresh cilantro
and chopped mint, 2 tablespoons olive oil, 2 finely
chopped garlic cloves, and season. Spoon over the
lamb, roll and skewer, then roast as above. **Calories
per serving 379**

seafood hotpot

Calories per serving **413**
Serves **4**
Preparation time **25 minutes**
Cooking time **15 minutes**

1 teaspoon **sesame oil**
1 tablespoon **vegetable oil**
3 **shallots**, chopped
3 **garlic cloves**, crushed
1 **onion**, sliced
²/₃ cup **coconut milk**
²/₃ cup **water**
3 tablespoons **rice wine vinegar**
1 **lemon grass stalk**, chopped
4 **kaffir lime leaves**
1 **red chile**, chopped
1¼ cups **fish stock** or **water**
1 tablespoon **sugar**
2 **tomatoes**, quartered
4 tablespoons **fish sauce**
1 teaspoon **tomato paste**
12 oz **straight-to-wok rice noodles**
12 oz **jumbo shrimp**, heads removed and peeled
4 oz **squid**, cleaned and cut into rings
6 oz **clams**, scrubbed
1 (15 oz) can **straw mushrooms**, drained
20 **basil leaves**

Heat the sesame and vegetable oils together in a large pan, add the shallots and garlic and sauté gently for 2 minutes or until softened but not browned.

Add the onion, coconut milk, measured water, vinegar, lemon grass, lime leaves, chile, stock or water, and sugar to the pan, bring to the boil and boil for 2 minutes. Reduce the heat and add the tomatoes, fish sauce, and tomato paste and cook for 5 minutes. Stir in the rice noodles.

Add the shrimp, squid rings, clams, and mushrooms to the hotpot and simmer gently for 5–6 minutes or until the seafood is cooked. Stir in the basil leaves. Serve the hotpot immediately.

For nuoc mam dipping sauce, to serve as an accompaniment, mix the following ingredients together: 6 tablespoons fish sauce, 2 teaspoons sugar, 1 tablespoon rice wine vinegar, 3 finely chopped hot red chiles, and 2 finely chopped hot green chiles. Let stand for 1 hour. **Calories per serving 25**

chicken wrapped in prosciutto

Calories per serving **431**
Serves **4**
Preparation time **10 minutes**
Cooking time **10 minutes**

4 boneless, skinless **chicken breasts**, about 5 oz each
4 slices of **prosciutto**
4 **sage leaves**
all-purpose flour, for dusting
2 tablespoons **butter**
2 tablespoons **olive oil**
4 sprigs **cherry tomatoes on the vine**
²/₃ cup **dry white wine**
salt and **pepper**

Lay each chicken breast between 2 sheets of plastic wrap and flatten with a rolling pin or meat mallet until wafer thin. Season with salt and pepper.

Lay a slice of prosciutto on each chicken breast, followed by a sage leaf. Secure the sage and ham in position with a toothpick, then lightly dust both sides of the chicken with flour. Season again with salt and pepper.

Heat the butter and oil in a large skillet over high heat, add the chicken and cook for 4–5 minutes on each side or until the juices run clear when pierced with a knife. Add the tomatoes and wine to the pan and bubble until the wine has thickened and reduced by about half. Serve immediately, accompanied by a green salad.

For veal scallops with rosemary & pancetta, take 4 veal scallops, about 5 oz each, and flatten as above. Top each flattened scallop with a sprinkling of rosemary leaves, then wrap each one in a slice of pancetta, instead of the prosciutto, omitting the sage. Dust with flour, season with salt and pepper, and cook as above. **Calories per serving 341**

trout with pesto

Calories per serving **422**
Serves **4**
Preparation time **10 minutes**
Cooking time **10 minutes**

¼ cup **olive oil**, plus extra for
    greasing
4 **trout tenderloins**, about
    7 oz each
large handful of **basil**, coarsely
    chopped, plus extra to
    garnish
1 **garlic clove**, crushed
½ cup freshly grated
    Parmesan cheese
salt and **pepper**
salad, to serve

Brush a baking sheet lightly with oil and place under
a preheated very hot broiler to heat up.

Put the trout tenderloins onto the hot sheet, sprinkle
with salt and pepper, and place under the broiler for
8–10 minutes, until lightly browned and the fish flakes
easily when pressed with a knife.

Meanwhile, put the basil and garlic into a bowl. Work
in the oil using an immersion blender, then stir in the
Parmesan cheese.

Remove the fish from the broiler, transfer to serving
plates, drizzle with the pesto, sprinkle with extra basil
leaves to garnish, and serve with salad.

For orange & almond trout, put the trout tenderloins
on a foil-lined broiler rack as above. Mix together the
finely grated zest and juice of 1 small orange,
1 tablespoon chopped parsley, and ¼ cup olive oil.
Brush the mixture over the tenderloins and season
with salt and pepper. Broil until golden and opaque,
then sprinkle with toasted sliced almonds. Serve with
a simple salad. **Calories per serving 403**

sesame-crusted salmon salad

Calories per serving **422**
Serves **4**
Preparation time **25 minutes**
Cooking time **4–10 minutes**

4 **scallions**
2 **egg whites**
1 tablespoon **white sesame seeds**
1 tablespoon **black sesame seeds**
1 lb **salmon tenderloin**
1 **frisée (curly-leaved chicory)**, divided into leaves
2 bunches of **watercress**
salt and **pepper**

Dressing
3 tablespoons **white wine vinegar**
5 tablespoons **vegetable oil**
1 tablespoon **sesame oil**
1 tablespoon **soy sauce**
1 teaspoon **sugar**
1 bunch of **chives**, finely chopped

Cut the scallions into thin strips and put them in cold water.

Lightly beat the egg whites. Mix the white and black sesame seeds with salt and pepper on a large plate. Dip the salmon tenderloin in the egg whites, then roll it in the sesame seeds. Pat the salmon on the seeds all over to give a good, even coating. Heat a ridged grill pan, add the salmon, and cook for 2 minutes each side for rare or 5 minutes for well done.

Make the dressing by mixing together the vinegar, oils, soy sauce, sugar, and chives. Toss the frisée leaves and watercress in the dressing. Arrange the leaves on a large serving dish.

Finely slice the salmon tenderloin and place on top of the salad. Drain the scallion curls, dry them on paper towels, and sprinkle over the salmon. Serve immediately.

For sashimi salmon salad, grate 1 raw beet and 2 carrots and mix with 2½ cups arugula. Make the dressing as above. Mix together 1 tablespoon each white and black sesame seeds. Slice as thinly as possible 2 skinless tenderloins of fresh salmon, each 5 oz, and arrange on individual plates. Drizzle the dressing over the salad, garnish with the sesame seeds, and serve with the salmon. **Calories per serving 338**

pepper-crusted loin of venison

Calories per serving **424**
Serves **4**
Preparation time **10 minutes**
Cooking time **30–45 minutes**

1 ½ lb **loin of venison**, cut
  from the haunch
¾ cup **mixed peppercorns**,
  crushed
2 tablespoons **juniper berries**,
  crushed
1 **egg white**, lightly beaten
salt and **pepper**

Make sure that the venison fits into your broiler pan;
if necessary, cut the loin in half to fit.

Mix together the peppercorns, juniper berries, and some
salt in a large, shallow dish. Dip the venison in the egg
white, then roll it in the peppercorn mixture, covering
it evenly all over.

Cook the venison under a preheated hot broiler for
4 minutes on each of the four sides, turning it carefully
so that the crust stays intact. Transfer the loin to a lightly
greased roasting pan and cook in a preheated oven,
400°F, for another 15 minutes for rare and up to
30 minutes for well done (the time will depend on the
thickness of the loin of venison).

Let the venison rest for a few minutes, then slice it
thickly and serve with green beans, red currant jelly,
and finely sliced sweet potato chips.

For Chinese-style venison steaks with bok choy,
omit the peppercorns and juniper berries and replace
the loin of venison with 4 x 6 oz venison steaks. Make
a marinade by mixing together 3 tablespoons soy
sauce, 1 tablespoon each finely grated fresh ginger root,
oyster sauce, and rice wine, 2 crushed garlic cloves, and
2 tablespoons peanut oil. Marinate for up to an hour,
then grill for 3–4 minutes on each side. Serve with
noodles and bok choy. **Calories per serving 429**

tuna enchiladas

Calories per serving **437**
Serves **4**
Preparation time **10 minutes**
Cooking time **15 minutes**

2 ripe **tomatoes**
1 **red onion**, peeled and finely
    chopped
1 tablespoon **lime juice** or
    to taste
8 **chapattis**
1 (10 oz) can **tuna in spring
    water**, drained
5 oz **reduced-fat cheddar
    cheese**, grated
salt and **pepper**
fresh cilantro, chopped,
    to garnish

Chop the tomatoes and mix them with the onion.
Season well and add lime juice to taste.

Spoon some of the tomato mixture over each
chapatti, top with the tuna and half the cheese. Roll up
each chapatti and arrange them in a heatproof dish.
Sprinkle over the remaining cheese and any remaining
tomato salsa.

Cover and cook in a preheated oven, 400°F, for
15 minutes, until golden. Garnish with cilantro and
serve immediately.

For veggie enchiladas, slice and broil 12 mushrooms
and 2 zucchini and and use instead of the tuna. For
extra spice, add a chopped and seeded jalapeño chile to
the tomatoes and onions. **Calories per serving 402**

chile pork with pineapple rice

Calories per serving **440**
Serves **4**
Preparation time **20 minutes,
    plus marinating**
Cooking time **15 minutes**

2 tablespoons **sunflower oil**
2 tablespoons **lime juice**
2 **garlic cloves**, crushed
1 **red chile**, seeded and finely
    chopped
10 oz **pork tenderloin**, cubed
1 cup **Thai fragrant rice**
6 **scallions**, finely sliced
1 cup diced **pineapple**
½ **red onion**, cut into wedges
1 **lime**, cut into wedges
salt and **pepper**
prepared **sweet chili sauce**,
    to serve

Presoak 8 wooden skewers in warm water.
Mix together the oil, lime juice, garlic, chile and salt
and pepper in a bowl, add the pork and stir to coat.
Cover and refrigerate for at least 1 hour.

Meanwhile, cook the rice in lightly salted boiling
water for 12–15 minutes or according to the
instructions on the package. Drain and stir through
the scallions and pineapple.

Thread the pork onto the skewers, alternating it with
onion and lime wedges, and cook under a preheated
hot broiler for about 10 minutes, turning frequently
and basting with the remaining marinade, until the
pork is cooked through.

Put the skewers and rice on a plate with the sweet
chili sauce and serve immediately.

For chile ham, replace the pork with 10 oz cubed ham
and use 1 green bell pepper, cut into wedges, instead
of the lime. When threading the ham onto the skewers,
alternate it with onion wedges and green pepper
wedges. Serve with mango chutney instead of sweet
chili sauce. **Calories per serving 454**

beef & flat noodle soup

Calories per serving **442**
Serves **6**
Preparation time **30 minutes**
Cooking time **2 hours**

1 tablespoon **vegetable oil**
1 lb **braising beef**
7 cups **beef stock**
4 **star anise**
1 **cinnamon stick**
1 teaspoon **black peppercorns**
4 **shallots**, thinly sliced
4 **garlic cloves**, crushed
3 inch piece of **fresh ginger root**, finely sliced
10 oz **flat rice noodles**
12 cup **bean sprouts**
6 **scallions**, thinly sliced
handful of **fresh cilantro**
8 oz **beef tenderloin**, sliced
2 tablespoons **fish sauce**
salt and **pepper**
hot red chilies, to garnish

Nuoc cham sauce
2 **red chilies**, chopped
1 **garlic clove**, chopped
1½ tablespoons **sugar**
1 tablespoon **lime juice**
1 tablespoon **rice wine vinegar**
3 tablespoons **fish sauce**

Heat the oil in a large saucepan or casserole and sear the beef on all sides until thoroughly brown.

Add the stock, star anise, cinnamon, black peppercorns, half the shallots, the garlic, and ginger. Bring to a boil, removing any scum. Reduce the heat, cover the pan with a lid and simmer very gently for about 1½ hours or until the beef is tender.

To make the nuoc cham sauce, pound the chiles, garlic, and sugar until smooth, using mortar and pestle. Add the lime juice, vinegar, fish sauce, and ¼ cup water and blend together well.

When the beef in the broth is tender, lift it out and slice it thinly. Add the noodles to the broth and cook gently for 2–3 minutes to soften. Add the bean sprouts along with the sliced beef and heat for 1 minute. Divide the broth, noodles, and bean sprouts among warmed serving bowls. Top with the beef, scallions, cilantro, and remaining shallots. Garnish with the chilies. Serve with the nuoc cham sauce.

For tofu and flat noodle soup, replace the beef with 8 oz tofu, cut into small squares and drained on paper towels. Sear as above. Replace the beef stock with the same quantity of vegetable stock and replace the fish sauce with the same quantity of soy sauce throughout. Reduce the cooking time to 20 minutes. Add 1 cup frozen edamame (soy) beans with the noodles. **Calories per serving 330**

swordfish with onion & golden raisins

Calories per serving 446
Serves **4**
Preparation time **10 minutes**
Cooking time **20 minutes**

¼ cup **olive oil**
1 **onion**, thinly sliced
1 **celery stick**, sliced
2 tablespoons **golden raisins**
1 **bay leaf**
3 tablespoons **pine nuts**
2 **garlic cloves**, sliced
4 **swordfish steaks**, about
    1 inch thick
all-purpose flour, seasoned
    with **salt** and **pepper**, for
    coating
⅔ cup **dry white wine**

Heat half the oil in a large, heavy skillet over low heat. Add the onion, celery, golden raisins, and bay leaf and cook for 8–10 minutes, until soft and golden. Stir in the pine nuts and garlic and cook for another 2 minutes. Remove to a dish.

Heat the remaining oil in the pan over high heat. Turn the swordfish steaks in the seasoned flour to coat on both sides. Add to the hot oil and cook for 3 minutes on each side until golden brown.

Return the onion mixture to the pan and pour in the wine. Boil vigorously for 2 minutes. Serve immediately.

For tuna with onion & olives, follow the first step above, but omit the raisins and replace the pine nuts with ⅓ cup halved, pitted black ripe olives. Continue with the recipe as above, but use 4 tuna steaks, about 1 inch thick, instead of the swordfish steaks. Calories per serving 423

sugar & spice salmon

Calories per serving **499**
Serves **4**
Preparation time **5 minutes**
Cooking time **10 minutes**

4 **salmon tenderloins**, about
  7 oz each
3 tablespoons packed **light
  brown sugar**
2 **garlic cloves**, crushed
1½ teaspoons **cumin seeds**,
  crushed
1 teaspoon smoked or ordinary
  paprika
1 tablespoon **white wine
  vinegar**
3 tablespoons **peanut oil**, plus
  extra for oiling
salt and **pepper**
2 **zucchini**, sliced into thin
  ribbons
lemon or **lime slices**, to serve

Put the salmon tenderloins in a lightly oiled roasting pan. Mix together the sugar, garlic, 1 teaspoon crushed cumin seeds, paprika, vinegar, and a little salt in a bowl, then spread the mixture all over the fish so that it is thinly coated. Drizzle with 1 tablespoon of oil.

Bake in a preheated oven, 425°F, for 10 minutes or until the fish is cooked through.

Heat the remaining oil in a large skillet, add the remaining crushed cumin seeds, and cook for 10 seconds. Add the zucchini ribbons, season with salt and pepper, and stir-fry for 2–3 minutes, until just softened.

Transfer to warm serving plates and serve the salmon on top, garnished with lemon or lime wedges.

For salmon with pesto crust, put the salmon in a lightly oiled roasting pan, season with pepper, and add a squeeze of lemon juice. Mix together ¼ cup pesto and 2 handfuls of fresh white bread crumbs in a bowl, then spread on top of the salmon. Grate Parmesan cheese over the top and drizzle with olive oil. Bake as above and serve with green beans and new potatoes.
Calories per serving 483

duck, clementine & tatsoi salad

Calories per serving **403**
Serves **4–6**
Preparation time **20 minutes**
Cooking time **15 minutes**

3 **duck breasts**, each about
    7½ oz
2½ cups **green beans**,
    trimmed
3 **clementines**, peeled and
    segmented
4 cups **tatsoi** or **spinach**

Dressing
juice of 2 **clementines**
1 tablespoon **white wine**
    vinegar
¼ cup **olive oil**
salt and **pepper**

Put the duck breasts, skin side down, in a cold ovenproof skillet and cook over medium heat for 6 minutes or until the skin has turned crisp and brown. Turn them over and cook for another 2 minutes. Transfer the duck to a preheated oven, 350°F, and cook for 5 minutes, until cooked through. Remove the duck breasts from the oven, cover with foil and let rest.

Meanwhile, blanch the green beans in lightly salted boiling water for 2 minutes, until cooked but still firm and bright green. Drain and refresh in cold water. Transfer the beans to a large salad bowl with the clementine segments.

Make the dressing by whisking together the clementine juice, vinegar, and oil in a small bowl. Season to taste with salt and pepper.

Add the tatsoi or spinach to the beans and clementines, drizzle over the dressing and combine well. Slice the duck meat, combine it with the salad, and serve immediately.

For orange & mustard dressing, an alternative dressing for this salad, cut 2 oranges in half and place them, flesh side down, on a hot ridged grill pan. Cook until they are charred and golden. Squeeze the orange juice into a small saucepan and reduce over medium heat for 5 minutes until slightly thickened. Whisk in 1 tablespoon whole-grain mustard and ¼ cup olive oil. Let cool slightly and serve warm.
Calories per serving 429

taverna-style grilled lamb with feta

Calories per serving **456**
Serves **4**
Preparation time **8 minutes**
Cooking time **6–8 minutes**

1 lb **leg** or **shoulder of lamb**,
  diced

Marinade
2 tablespoons chopped
  oregano
1 tablespoon chopped
  rosemary
grated zest of 1 **lemon**
2 tablespoons **olive oil**
salt and **pepper**

Feta salad
7 oz **feta cheese**, sliced
1 tablespoon chopped
  oregano
2 tablespoons chopped
  parsley
grated zest and juice of
1 **lemon**
½ small **red onion**, finely
  sliced
3 tablespoons **olive oil**

Mix together the marinade ingredients in a nonmetallic bowl, add the lamb, and mix to coat thoroughly. Thread the meat onto 4 skewers.

Arrange the sliced feta on a large serving dish and sprinkle with the herbs, lemon zest and sliced onion. Drizzle over the lemon juice and oil and season with salt and pepper.

Cook the lamb skewers under a preheated hot broiler or in a ridged grill pan for about 6–8 minutes, turning frequently until browned and almost cooked through. Remove from heat and let rest for 1–2 minutes.

Serve the lamb, with any pan juices poured over, with the feta salad.

For pork with red cabbage, replace the lamb with the same quantity of lean, boneless pork. Marinate and cook the pork as above. Replace the feta with 8 oz finely chopped red cabbage. Omit the oregano and swap the lemon for an orange. Mix the ingredients together and marinate for 5 minutes before serving.
Calories per serving 313

lime & coconut squid

Calories per serving **452**
Serves **2**
Preparation time **15 minutes**
Cooking time **5 minutes**

10–12 prepared **baby squid**,
   about 12 oz including
   tentacles, cleaned
4 **limes**, halved

Dressing
2 **red chiles**, deseeded and
   finely chopped
finely grated zest and juice of
   2 **limes**
1 inch piece of **fresh ginger
   root**, peeled and grated
1 cup freshly grated **coconut**
¼ cup **peanut oil**
1–2 tablespoons **chili oil**
1 tablespoon **white wine
   vinegar**

Cut down the side of each squid so that they can be laid flat on a chopping board. Using a sharp knife, lightly score the inside flesh in a crisscross pattern.

Mix all the dressing ingredients together in a bowl. Toss the squid in half the dressing until thoroughly coated.

Heat a ridged grill pan until smoking hot, add the limes, cut side down, and cook for 2 minutes or until well charred. Remove from the pan and set aside. Keeping the grill pan very hot, add the squid pieces and cook for 1 minute. Turn them over and cook for another minute or until they turn white, lose their transparency, and are charred.

Transfer the squid to a chopping board and cut into strips. Drizzle with the remaining dressing and serve immediately with the charred limes and a salad of mixed green leaves.

For lemon & garlic squid, remove the tentacles from the prepared squid and slice the bodies into rings. Place in a nonmetallic dish with the juice of 1 lemon and let marinate for 5 minutes. Heat ⅓ cup olive oil in a large skillet and add 3 chopped garlic cloves and the grated zest of 1 lemon. When the oil is very hot, add the squid and cook over high heat for 1–2 minutes or until it turns white and loses its transparency. Season with salt and pepper and serve sprinkled with parsley and with lemon wedges on the side. **Calories per serving 379**

angler fish with beans & pesto

Calories per serving **455**

Serves **4**

Preparation time **10 minutes**

Cooking time **10–15 minutes**

1 lb **angler fish**, cut into 12 pieces

12 slices of **prosciutto**

12 **cherry tomatoes**

2 **yellow bell peppers**, cored, seeded, and cut into 6 wedges

2 tablespoons **olive oil**

1 cup rinsed and drained canned **cannellini beans**

¼ cup **prepared pesto**

Presoak 4 wooden skewers in warm water. Wrap each piece of angler fish in a slice of prosciutto. Thread these on to skewers, alternating with tomatoes and pieces of yellow pepper. Brush the kebabs with the oil and cook under a preheated hot broiler for 3–4 minutes. Turn the skewers over and cook for another 3 minutes, until cooked through.

Put the beans in a nonstick saucepan and cook, stirring, over low heat for 4–5 minutes or until hot. Stir in the pesto. Spoon the beans onto 4 plates, top with the kebabs and serve immediately.

For scallops with green beans & pesto, replace the angler fish with 16 scallops, wrap each one in a piece of prosciutto and skewer as above, omitting the peppers. Broil as above. Replace the cannellini beans with 2 cups green beans and cook as above. Serve immediately, with crusty French bread on the side. **Calories per serving 375**

lamb with tangy lima beans

Calories per serving **456**

Serves **2**

Preparation time **10 minutes**

Cooking time **10 minutes**

2 tablespoons finely chopped **mint**

1 tablespoon finely chopped **thyme**

1 tablespoon finely chopped **oregano**

½ tablespoon finely chopped **rosemary**

4 teaspoons **whole-grain mustard**

4 **lamb chops**, about 4 oz each

Tangy lima beans

2 teaspoons **vegetable oil**

1 **onion**, chopped

1 tablespoon **tomato paste**

3 tablespoons **pineapple juice**

2 tablespoons **lemon juice**

a few drops of **Tabasco sauce**

1 cup canned **lima beans**, drained

pepper

Mix together all the chopped herbs on a plate. Spread mustard on both sides of each chop, then press into the herb mixture to coat evenly.

Make the tangy lima beans. Heat the oil in a skillet, add the onion, and cook gently for 5 minutes. Add the remaining ingredients to the pan and cook gently for 5 minutes.

Meanwhile, secure the thin end of the lamb around the base with a toothpick. Place on a foil-lined broiler pan and cook under a preheated hot broiler for 4 minutes on each side or until cooked but still slightly pink in the center. Serve immediately, surrounded by the tangy lima beans.

For lamb chops wrapped in prosciutto, mix together 1 tablespoon finely chopped drained capers, 1 crushed garlic clove, ½ tablespoon chopped rosemary, the grated zest of ½ lemon, and 1 tablespoon olive oil in a nonmetallic shallow dish. Add the lamb chops and toss to coat in the marinade. Season well, cover and let marinate in the refrigerator for at least 20 minutes. Fold 4 slices of prosciutto lengthwise, then wrap around the edge of each of the chops. Heat 1 tablespoon vegetable oil in an ovenproof skillet and brown the prosciutto edges of the chops, then seal each side of the lamb briefly. Cook in a preheated oven, 400°F, for 12–15 minutes or until cooked but still slightly pink in the center. Remove from the oven and let rest before serving.
Calories per serving 395

salmon with lime zucchini

Calories per serving **463**
Serves **4**
Preparation time **10 minutes**
Cooking time **10–15 minutes**

4 **salmon tenderloin** portions,
  about 7 oz each
1 tablespoon prepared
  English mustard
½ inch piece of **fresh ginger
  root**, peeled and finely
  grated
1 teaspoon crushed **garlic**
2 teaspoons **honey**
1 tablespoon **light soy sauce**
  or **tamari**
salt and **pepper**

Lime zucchini
2 tablespoons **olive oil**
1 lb **zucchini**, thinly sliced
  lengthwise
grated zest and juice of **1 lime**
2 tablespoons chopped **mint**

Lay the salmon tenderloin portions, skin side down, in
a shallow flameproof dish, to fit snugly in a single layer.
In a small bowl, mix together the mustard, ginger, garlic,
honey, and soy sauce or tamari, then spoon evenly over
the tenderloins. Season to taste with salt and pepper.

Heat the broiler on the hottest setting. Cook the salmon
tenderloins under the broiler for 10–15 minutes, until
lightly charred on top and cooked through.

Meanwhile, to prepare the lime zucchini, heat the oil
in a large nonstick skillet, add the zucchini, and cook,
stirring frequently, for 5–6 minutes or until lightly
browned and tender. Stir in the lime zest and juice
and mint and season to taste with salt and pepper.

Serve the salmon hot with the zucchini.

For stir-fried green beans to serve in place of the
lime zucchini, cut 1 lb green beans into 2 inch lengths.
Heat 2 tablespoons vegetable oil in a wok or large
skillet, add 2 crushed garlic cloves, 1 teaspoon grated
fresh ginger root, and 2 thinly sliced shallots and stir-fry
over medium heat for 1 minute. Add the beans and
½ teaspoon salt and stir-fry over high heat for 1 minute.
Add 1 tablespoon light soy sauce and ⅔ cup chicken
or vegetable stock and bring to a boil. Reduce the heat
and cook, stirring frequently, for another 4 minutes, or
until the beans are tender and the liquid has thickened.
Season with pepper and serve immediately with the
salmon. **Calories per serving 482**

chickpeas with chorizo

Calories per serving **461**
Serves **4**
Preparation time **10 minutes**
Cooking time **about
  10 minutes**

2 tablespoons **olive oil**
1 **red onion**, finely chopped
2 **garlic cloves**, crushed
7 oz **chorizo sausage**, cut into
  ½ inch dice
2 ripe **tomatoes**, seeded and
  finely chopped
3 tablespoons chopped
  parsley
2 (15 oz) cans **chickpeas**,
  drained
salt and **pepper**

Heat the oil in a large nonstick skillet, add the onion, garlic, and chorizo and cook over medium-high heat, stirring frequently, for 4–5 minutes.

Add the tomatoes, parsley, and chickpeas to the pan and cook, stirring frequently, for 4–5 minutes or until heated through.

Season to taste with salt and pepper and serve immediately or let cool to room temperature. Serve with crusty bread, if desired.

For harissa-spiced chickpeas with haloumi & spinach, heat the oil in a large saucepan, add 2 chopped onions and the garlic, omitting the chorizo, and cook over low heat until softened. Omit the fresh tomatoes and parsley and add 2 tablespoons harissa paste, the chickpeas, and 2 (14½ oz) cans diced tomatoes to the pan. Bring to a boil, then reduce the heat and simmer for about 5 minutes. Add 8 oz cubed haloumi cheese and 4 cups baby leaf spinach and cook over low heat for another 5 minutes. Season to taste with salt and pepper and stir in the juice of 1 lemon. Serve with grated Parmesan cheese and warm crusty bread. **Calories per serving 470**

salmon & bulgur wheat pilaf

Calories per serving **478**
Serves **4**
Preparation time **10 minutes**
Cooking time **10–15 minutes**

15 oz boneless, skinless **salmon**
1 ¼ cups **bulgur wheat**
½ cup frozen **peas**
7 oz **runner beans** or **green beens**, chopped
2 tablespoons chopped **chives**
2 tablespoons chopped **flat-leaf parsley**
salt and **pepper**

To serve
2 **lemons**, halved
low-fat yogurt

Cook the salmon in a steamer or microwave for about 10 minutes. Alternatively, wrap it in foil and cook in a preheated oven, 350°F, for 15 minutes.

Meanwhile, cook the bulgur wheat according to the instructions on the package and boil the peas and beans. Alternatively, cook the bulgur wheat, peas, and beans in the steamer with the salmon.

Flake the salmon and mix it into the bulgur wheat with the peas and beans. Fold in the chives and parsley and season with salt and pepper to taste. Serve immediately with lemon halves and yogurt.

For ham & bulgur wheat pilaf, pan-fry 10 oz diced lean ham instead of the salmon. Replace the runner beans with the same quantity of fava beans and fold in 2 tablespoons chopped mint along with the chives and parsley. **Calories per serving 450**

teriyaki beef with rice noodles

Calories per serving **480**
Preparation time **15 minutes,
    plus marinating**
Cooking time **10 minutes**
Serves **4**

1 lb **sirloin steak**
9 oz **dried rice ribbon
    noodles**
2 teaspoons **sesame oil**
1 inch piece of **fresh ginger
    root**, peeled and finely
    grated
1 **garlic clove**, finely sliced
1 cup **snow peas**, sliced
1 **carrot**, cut into matchsticks
4 **scallions**, shredded
handful of **cilantro**, chopped

Teriyaki marinade
2 tablespoons **soy sauce**
2 tablespoons **sake**
1 tablespoon **mirin**
½ tablespoon **sugar**

Make the marinade by mixing together all the ingredients in a small bowl. Place the beef in a dish, pour over the marinade, cover and marinate in the refrigerator for at least 2 hours, preferably overnight.

Soak the rice noodles in boiling water according to the package instructions. Drain well.

Preheat a ridged grill pan, meanwhile, so it is really hot. Place the beef on the pan, reserving the marinade, and cook for 2–3 minutes on each side. Transfer to a chopping board and let rest.

Heat the oil in a wok or large skillet, add the ginger and garlic and cook for 30 seconds. Add the vegetables and cook until just beginning to soften.

Add the cilantro, noodles, and 2–3 tablespoons of the marinade and heat through. Spoon onto 4 serving plates, slice the beef, and serve on top of the noodles.

For Thai beef salad, mix together the marinade ingredients as above, adding 1 teaspoon sesame oil, the grated zest and juice of 1 lime, 3 tablespoons Thai fish sauce, a handful each of chopped cilantro, mint, and Thai basil. Cover and chill. When ready to serve, grill the beef as above. Using a peeler, slice ½ cucumber and 2 carrots into ribbons and stir into the chilled dressing with 4 shredded scallions, 12 halved cherry tomatoes, and 5 cups salad greens. Slice the steak thinly, stir into the salad and serve. **Calories per serving 296**

trout with cucumber relish

Calories per serving **424**
Serves **4**
Preparation time **10 minutes**
Cooking time **10–12 minutes**

4 **rainbow trout**, cleaned and
   gutted
1 tablespoon **sesame oil**
crushed **Szechuan pepper**,
   to taste
salt
chopped **chives**, to garnish
lemon wedges, to serve

For the cucumber relish
1 **cucumber**, about 8 inches
   long
2 teaspoons **salt**
¼ cup **rice vinegar**
3 tablespoons **caster sugar**
1 **red chile**, deseeded and
   sliced
1 ¼ inch piece of **fresh ginger
   root**, peeled and grated
¼ cup **cold water**

Make the cucumber relish. Cut the cucumber in half
lengthwise, scoop out and discard the seeds and cut
the flesh into ½ inch slices. Put in a glass or ceramic
bowl. In a small bowl, put the salt, vinegar, sugar, chile,
and ginger, add the water, and mix well. Pour over the
cucumber, cover, and let marinate at room temperature
while you cook the trout.

Brush the trout with the oil and season to taste with
crushed Szechuan pepper and salt. Place the trout in a
single layer on a broiler rack and broil for 5–6 minutes
on each side or until cooked through. Let rest for a few
moments, then garnish with chopped chives and serve
with the cucumber relish and lemon wedges.

For trout with chestnut dressing, brush the trout
with 1 teaspoon olive oil and season to taste with salt
and black pepper. While the trout is cooking as above,
put ¾ cup peeled chestnuts in a small saucepan over
medium heat and cook, stirring constantly, until lightly
browned. Remove from the heat, add ¼ cup olive oil,
3 tablespoons lemon juice, and 2 tablespoons chopped
parsley, and season to taste with salt and pepper. Stir
well, then return to the heat for 2 minutes. Pour the
dressing over the cooked trout, garnish with parsley sprigs,
and serve immediately. **Calories per serving 499**

214

salmon & puy lentils with parsley

Calories per serving **486**
Serves **4**
Preparation time **15 minutes**
Cooking time **35 minutes**

1 cup **Puy lentils**
1 **bay leaf**
2 cups fine **green beans**,
   chopped
1 cup chopped **flat-leaf
   parsley**
2 tablespoons **Dijon mustard**
2 tablespoons **capers**, rinsed
   and chopped
2 tablespoons **olive oil**
2 **lemons**, finely sliced
about 1 lb **salmon
   tenderloins**
1 **fennel bulb**, finely sliced
salt and **pepper**
dill sprigs, to garnish

Put the lentils into a saucepan with the bay leaf and
enough cold water to cover (do not add salt). Bring to
a boil, reduce to a simmer, and cook for 30 minutes or
until tender. Season with salt and pepper to taste, add
the beans and simmer for 1 minute. Drain the lentils
and stir in the parsley, mustard, capers, and oil. Discard
the bay leaf.

Meanwhile, arrange the lemon slices on a foil-lined
broiler pan and put the salmon and fennel slices on
top. Season the salmon and fennel and cook under
a preheated hot broiler for about 10 minutes or until
the salmon is cooked through.

Serve the fennel slices and lentils with the salmon on
top, garnished with dill sprigs.

For pork scallops with lentils, prepare the Puy
lentils as above and replace the salmon with 4 pork
scallops. Broil the pork as above, omitting the fennel.
Meanwhile, finely slice 2 celery sticks and toss with
a little walnut oil. Serve the lentils with the scallops on
top, garnished with the celery and walnut oil. **Calories
per serving 437**

beef in red wine

Calories per serving **490**
  **(not including potatoes or
  polenta)**
Serves **4**
Preparation time **10 minutes**
Cooking time **2¼ hours**

1¾ lb **brisket of beef**, cut into
  2 inch pieces
1 **celery stick**, sliced
2 **bay leaves**
1 bottle **Barolo** or other full-
  bodied **red wine**
1¼ cups **beef** or **chicken
  stock**
2 **carrots**, cut at an angle into
  1½ inch slices
20 **baby onions**, peeled but
  kept whole
salt and **pepper**

Season the beef with salt and pepper and put in
a large, flameproof casserole with a tight-fitting lid.
Add the celery and bay leaves, then pour in the wine
and stock. Bring to a boil, then reduce the heat to a
barely visible simmer and cook, covered, for 1½ hours,
stirring occasionally.

Add the carrots and onions. Replace the lid and simmer
gently for another 45 minutes, adding a little water if
the sauce becomes too thick.

Remove the beef from the heat and serve with mashed
potatoes or soft polenta, if desired.

For oxtail in red wine with tomatoes, replace the
beef with 4 lb oxtail chunks. Cook as above, adding
1 (14½ oz) can diced tomatoes and reducing the red
wine to 1½ cups. Simmer gently for 2½ hours. Oxtail
releases a lot of fat, so ideally make the stew a day
ahead, let cool completely, then refrigerate. Skim off
all the solidified layer of fat before reheating. **Calories
per serving 463**

mussels with cider

Calories per serving **490 (not including French bread)**
Serves **2**
Preparation time **10 minutes**
Cooking time **9 minutes**

3 lb small **farmed mussels**
2 **garlic cloves**, chopped
2/3 cups **hard cider**
6 tablespoons **heavy cream**
2 tablespoons chopped **parsley**
salt and **black pepper**

Wash the mussels thoroughly, discarding any that do not close when tapped and put in a large saucepan with the garlic and cider. Bring to a boil, cover and cook over medium heat for 4–5 minutes until all the shells have opened. Discard any that remain closed after cooking.

Strain the mussels through a colander and put in a large bowl, cover with foil, and place in a very low oven to keep warm.

Pass the cooking juices through a fine-mesh strainer into a clean saucepan and bring to a boil. Whisk in the cream and simmer for 3–4 minutes or until thickened slightly. Season to taste with salt and pepper.

Pour the sauce over the mussels, sprinkle with the parsley and serve immediately with plenty of crusty French bread to mop up the juices, if desired.

For mussels with Asian flavors, wash the mussels thoroughly, discarding any that do not close when tapped and put in a large saucepan with 2 sliced garlic cloves, 2 teaspoons grated fresh ginger root, 4 sliced scallions, and 1 sliced red chile. Add a splash of water and cook as above. Strain the mussels and keep warm. Strain the cooking juices through a fine-mesh strainer into a clean saucepan. Whisk in 6 tablespoons coconut cream and heat through. Pour over the mussels and served garnished with chopped fresh cilantro. **Calories per serving 314**

lima bean & chorizo stew

Calories per serving **470**
Preparation time **10 minutes**
Cooking time **20 minutes**
Serves **4**

1 tablespoon **olive oil**
1 large **onion**, chopped
2 **garlic cloves**, crushed
7 oz **chorizo sausage**, sliced
1 **green bell pepper**, cored,
   seeded, and chopped
1 **red bell pepper**, cored,
   seeded, and chopped
1 glass **red wine**
2 x (15 oz) cans **lima beans**,
   drained and rinsed
1 (14½ oz) can **cherry
tomatoes**
1 tablespoon **tomato paste**
salt and **black pepper**
chopped **parsley**, to garnish
crusty bread, to serve

Heat the oil in a flameproof casserole, add the onion and garlic and cook for 1–2 minutes. Stir in the chorizo and fry until beginning to brown. Add the peppers and cook for 3 minutes.

Pour in the wine and allow to bubble, then stir in the lima beans, tomatoes, and tomato paste and season well with salt and pepper. Cover and simmer for 15 minutes. Ladle into shallow bowls, sprinkle with the parsley to garnish, and serve with crusty bread, if desired.

For garlic shrimp with lima beans, cook the onion and garlic as above, then stir in 10 oz raw peeled and deveined jumbo shrimp instead of the chorizo and fry until they just turn pink. Add the lima beans, 3 tablespoons light crème fraîche or sour cream and 2 handfuls of arugula leaves and season well. Heat through and serve. **Calories per serving 243**

grilled tuna salad

Calories per serving **451**
Serves **4**
Preparation time **10 minutes**
Cooking time **15 minutes**

1 lb small **new potatoes**,
   scrubbed
4 fresh **tuna steaks**, about
   6 oz each
2 cups **baby spinach leaves**,
   coarsely chopped
¼ cup **olive oil**
2 tablespoons **balsamic
   vinegar**
salt and **pepper**
griddled **lime wedges**,
   to serve

Place the new potatoes in a steamer over boiling water and cook for 15 minutes or until tender.

Meanwhile, heat a ridged grill pan. Pat the tuna tenderloins dry with paper towels and cook in the pan for 3 minutes on each side for rare, 5 minutes for medium, or 8 minutes for well done.

Remove the potatoes from the steamer. Slice them in half and place in a bowl. Add the spinach, olive oil, and balsamic vinegar. Toss and season to taste. Divide the salad among 4 plates and serve with a slice of tuna arranged on the top of each, and a griddled lime wedge for squeezing.

For warm Niçoise salad, cook the potatoes and tuna as above. Halve and blanch 1 cup fine beans and quickly fry ½ cup cherry tomatoes. Add the beans and tomatoes and ⅔ cup black ripe olives to the halved warm potatoes and spinach leaves. Flake the tuna and add to the salad. Season well and serve.
Calories per serving 496

shrimp, pea shoot & quinoa salad

Calories per serving **492**
Serves **4**
Preparation time **10 minutes**
Cooking time **10 minutes**

1½ cups **quinoa**
¾ cup **snow peas**, blanched
  and halved
7 oz **asparagus spears**,
  cooked, cooled, and cut into
  bite-size pieces
1¼ cups **pea shoots**
13 oz cooked **jumbo shrimp**,
  shells removed
salt and **pepper**

Fruit and nut dressing
2 tablespoons **olive oil**
2 tablespoons **lemon juice**
3 tablespoons **dried
  cranberries**
⅓ cup **hazelnuts**, chopped
  and toasted

Cook the quinoa according to the instructions on
the package. Set aside to cool.

Stir the snow peas and asparagus through the quinoa.

Make the dressing by mixing together the oil, lemon
juice, cranberries, and hazelnuts.

Spoon the pea shoots and shrimp over the quinoa,
drizzle over the dressing, and serve.

For shrimp, bulgur wheat & nut salad, use
1½ cups bulgur wheat instead of the quinoa.
For a nuttier dressing, toast ½ cup sliced almonds
in a dry pan with the hazelnuts, then mix with the
olive oil and the zest and juice of 1 orange.
Calories per serving 485

quick prosciutto & arugula pizza

Calories per serving **498**
Serves **4**
Preparation time **10 minutes**
Cooking time **10 minutes**

4 mini **pizza bases**
2 **garlic cloves**, halved
8 oz **reduced-fat mozzarella
   cheese**, shredded
8 **cherry tomatoes**, quartered
5 oz **prosciutto**, sliced
1¼ cups **arugula leaves**,
   washed
balsamic vinegar, to taste
salt and **pepper**

Rub the top surfaces of the pizza bases with the cut faces of the garlic cloves.

Put the pizza bases on a baking sheet, top with mozzarella and tomatoes, and bake in a preheated oven, 400°F, for 10 minutes, until the bread is golden.

Top the pizzas with slices of prosciutto and arugula leaves, season to taste with salt, pepper, and balsamic vinegar and serve immediately.

For tuna & pineapple pizza, drain and chop 1 (8 oz) can pineapple, and drain and flake 1 (5½ oz) can tuna in spring water. Top the pizza bases with the pineapple and tuna, then arrange the mozzarella and tomatoes over before cooking as above. **Calories per serving 481**

blackened salmon with salsa

Calories per serving **496**
Serves **4**
Preparation time **15 minutes**
Cooking time **8 minutes**

3 tablespoons **Cajun
  seasoning**
1 teaspoon **dried oregano**
4 **salmon tenderloins**, about
  3 oz each
sunflower oil, to brush
lime wedges, to garnish

Cajun salsa
1 (15 oz) can **black-eyed
  peas**, rinsed and drained
2 tablespoons **olive oil**
1 **avocado**, peeled, pitted and
  chopped
2 **plum tomatoes**, finely
  chopped
1 **yellow bell pepper**, seeded
  and finely chopped
2 tablespoons **lime juice**
salt and **pepper**

Mix together the Cajun seasoning and oregano in a
shallow bowl.

Brush the salmon on both sides with a little oil and
coat with the spice mix, making sure the fish is
completely covered. Set aside.

Meanwhile, make the salsa by mixing together all the
ingredients in a bowl. Season with salt and pepper to
taste and set aside.

Cook the salmon in a preheated, dry skillet for
4 minutes on each side.

Slice the salmon and serve with the salsa, with lime
wedges to garnish.

For salsa verde, drain and finely chop 6 anchovy
tenderloins in oil and combine them with 3 tablespoons
chopped basil, 3 tablespoons chopped parsley or
chives, 2 teaspoons coarsely chopped capers,
2 teaspoons Dijon mustard, 3 tablespoons olive oil,
and 1 ½ tablespoons white wine vinegar.
Calories per serving 335

cambodian fish pot

Calories per serving **499**
Serves **4**
Preparation time **10 minutes**
Cooking time **15 minutes**

1 teaspoon **sesame oil**
1 tablespoon **vegetable oil**
3 **shallots**, chopped
3 **garlic cloves**, crushed
1 **onion**, halved and sliced
2½ cups canned **coconut milk**
3 tablespoons **rice wine vinegar**
1 **lemon grass stalk**, chopped
4 **kaffir lime leaves**
3–6 **red Thai chiles**, halved and seeds removed
1¼ cups **fish stock**
1 tablespoon **sugar**
2 **tomatoes**, quartered
2 tablespoons **fish sauce**
1 teaspoon **tomato paste**
6 oz **live clams**, cleaned
12 oz raw peeled **jumbo shrimp**
4 oz **squid**, cleaned and cut into rings
1 (15 oz) can **straw mushrooms**, drained
20 **holy basil leaves** (optional)

Heat the sesame and vegetable oils together in a large flameproof casserole, add the shallots and garlic and sauté gently for 2 minutes or until softened but not browned.

Add the onion, coconut milk, rice wine vinegar, lemon grass, lime leaves, chiles, stock, and sugar to the casserole and bring to a boil. Boil for 2 minutes, then reduce the heat and add the tomatoes, fish sauce and tomato paste and cook for 5 minutes.

Discard any clams that don't shut when tapped, then add them with the shrimp, squid rings, and mushrooms to the casserole and simmer gently for 5–6 minutes or until the shrimp turn pink, the squid are cooked through, and the clams have opened. Discard any clams that remain closed. Stir in the basil leaves, if desired.

Serve the hotpot immediately with rice noodles.

For traditional fisherman's stew, replace the sesame and vegetable oils with olive oil and fry the garlic and shallots as above. When adding the onion, replace the coconut milk, rice wine vinegar, lemon grass, lime leaves, chiles, stock, and sugar with 2 (14½ oz) cans diced tomatoes, 1 pinch saffron threads, 1¼ cups white wine, and 1¼ lb white fish tenderloins, skinned and cut into bite-size chunks. Continue as above, adding the tomatoes, fish sauce, and tomato paste, then the shrimp, squid rings, and mushrooms, but replace the basil leaves with chopped parsley. Serve with crusty bread instead of the noodles, dipping sauce, and fresh cilantro. **Calories per serving 393**

roast pork with fennel

Calories per serving **451**
Serves **4**
Preparation time **10 minutes**
Cooking time **30 minutes**

1 ¼ lb **pork tenderloin**
1 large **rosemary sprig**,
   broken into short lengths,
   plus extra sprigs to garnish
3 **garlic cloves**, peeled and
   sliced
¼ cup **olive oil**
1 large **fennel bulb**, trimmed
   and cut into wedges, central
   core removed
1 large **red onion**, cut into
   wedges
1 large **red bell pepper**,
   halved, seeded, and cut
   into chunks
⅔ cup **white wine**
3 oz **mascarpone cheese**
   (optional)
salt and **pepper**

Pierce the pork with a sharp knife and insert the pieces of rosemary and garlic evenly all over the meat. Heat half the oil in a roasting pan on the stove, add the pork and cook for 5 minutes or until browned all over.

Add the fennel, onion, and red pepper to the roasting pan and drizzle the vegetables with the remaining oil. Season well with salt and pepper. Roast in a preheated oven, 450°F, for 20 minutes or until the juices run clear when the pork is pierced in the center with a knife.

Transfer the pork and vegetables to a serving plate and keep hot in the oven. Add the wine to the roasting pan and simmer on the stove until slightly reduced. Stir in the mascarpone, if using.

Cut the pork into slices and arrange on serving plates with spoonfuls of the roasted vegetables and a spoonful or two of the sauce. Serve immediately garnished with rosemary sprigs.

For roast pork with apples & cider sauce, pierce the pork, flavor with rosemary, and brown as above. Thickly slice 6 apples with assorted color skins. Heat 2 teaspoons butter and 1 tablespoon olive oil in a large skillet and fry the onion, red pepper, and apples for 4–5 minutes over moderately high heat until golden and soft. Transfer to a roasting pan, arrange the pork on top and roast as above. Keep the meat and vegetables warm. Make the sauce as above with ⅔ cup hard cider instead of wine and reduce before stirring in the mascarpone and 1 teaspoon Dijon mustard. Season to taste and serve as above. **Calories per serving 499**

index

acknowledgments

Commissioning editor: Eleanor Maxfield
Senior editor: Elinor Smith
Editor: Pollyanna Poulter
Art direction and design: Eoghan O'Brian
Production controller: Allison Gonsalves
Americanizer: Nicole Foster

All photos © Octopus Publishing Group

Stephen Conroy 11, 18, 23, 31, 53, 75, 79, 107, 110, 113, 141, 143, 155, 159, 169, 179, 193, 195, 199, 201, 205, 209, 215, 219, 233; Will Heap 15, 25, 41, 59, 61, 81, 93, 101, 133, 147, 181, 235; William Lingwood 29, 69, 203; David Loftus 177, 191; Neil Mersh 207; David Munns 163; Sean Myers 225; Lis Parsons 1, 2, 5, 6, 9, 12, 16, 33, 45, 65, 83, 91, 95, 97, 103, 115, 123, 127, 129, 137, 149, 151, 157, 161, 165, 173, 175, 187, 189, 197, 211, 217, 227, 229, 231; William Reavell 21, 37, 49, 125; Gareth Sambidge 63, 73, 117, 185; William Shaw 14, 39, 43, 47, 51, 77, 85, 89, 99, 105, 109, 121, 135, 145, 153, 213, 223; EleanorSkan 67, 87; Simon Smith 13, 27, 57; Ian Wallace 8, 10, 35, 55, 71, 119, 131, 139, 171, 221; Philip Webb 183